STAMP COUNTERFEITING

The Evolution of an Unrecognized Crime

By H.K. Petschel

 HKP PUBLICATIONS
Sandpoint, Idaho

© 2011 by H.K. Petschel

HKP Publications
70 Cedar Dr.
Sandpoint, ID 83864

Printed in the United States of America
Stamp Counterfeiting: The Evolution of an Unrecognized Crime

ISBN 978-0-615-50885-6

Cover design by Laura Wahl, text design by Christine Barrett, Keokee Co. Publishing, Inc. (www.keokee.com)

To Kitty Wonderly, the editor and midwife of my first book *Spurious Stamps* and various articles published by the American Philatelic Society. I had no idea of what she went through until I went through this hands-on experience of self-publishing with Keokee Co. Publishing Inc. My thanks to them for leading me through the rocks and shoals.

Thanks, as always, to the many individuals in the philatelic world who shared their knowledge and materials for my ongoing research.

This book is also dedicated to the men and women of the U.S. Secret Service and U.S. Postal Inspection Service who, through their dedication, protect us all.

CONTENTS

STAMP COUNTERFEITING

Preface

For me, this is how it all began.

Stamps are fascinating little bits of paper. Like virtually everyone who suffers from this addiction, my interest began as a child. It began when looking at a particular stamp one day and I suddenly realized it was counterfeit. This discovery would only generate more questions. Who made it, and why? Was its purpose to defraud some innocent collector, or was the target some government? Somewhere along the line I must have wondered why anyone would do this. Could people really make money counterfeiting stamps?

My interest in stamps was not a factor in my becoming a postal inspector. Once there, however, when not chasing mail thieves and robbers, I soon found my way into the investigation of postage frauds of all varieties. Postal counterfeiting, philatelic fraud, meter and mail house operations – to one degree or another – all caught my interest.

As an inspector, it was postal counterfeits – stamps made to defraud the government – that became an obsession. Being stationed in Chicago only aggravated this itch. Besides being centrally located, Chicago was a hot bed of both stamp and currency counterfeiting. Then, when I had to give testimony in court, first as an investigator and later as an authority, it seemed like a good idea to learn everything I could about this subject.

In a sense that is where the fun really began. Investigating my own cases had been easy. It was when one tried to piece together a historical record that the nightmare began. With the Postal Inspection Service, little historical documentation could be found in the files. Broken into geographic divisions, each one was a self-contained unit. Little information was shared across division lines, and what was reported to Washington is soon filed and forgotten. Here and there you might find bits and pieces, but that was all. To find out what had happened in the past, I had to go back to old newspapers, police name checks, and the National Archives. Inquiries to the Secret Service mostly went unanswered.

For a number of reasons I began to write about counterfeiting cases in the 1970s. First, I wanted to protect the historical record before these stories slipped further into the mist of time. Secondly, just maybe, my stories could have some small effect on how both the public, and especially official Washington, might look at this crime.

Initially, protecting postal revenue and combating postal counterfeiting played a large role in the thinking of postal administrators across the world. As time went by, the reasons why certain things were done were forgotten. Not surprisingly, when you have no historical context, and have forgotten why you were originally doing something, it is customary for administrators to put the emphasis on cutting costs. You forget there was a reason why stamps had grills, watermarks and perforations.

In frustration, on more than one occasion I concluded the motto for the post office should be:

If you do not look for counterfeits, you will not find them.
If you have not found counterfeits, they must not exist.
If they do not exist, you obviously do not have a problem.
If you do not have a problem, you do not have to look for them.

This is not a criticism of postal administrators, inspectors, or the public in general. It is simply human nature reacting to the real world. It's called watching the bottom line.

What I hope to do here is not simply a reprint of *Spurious Stamps* published by the American Philatelic Society in 1996. Ever since that book came out, I have wanted to go back and revisit the tales that were told. Yes, I am relating stamp stories, but they are so much more. What you will find are everyday crimes being committed by individuals trying to make a few bucks. You will also encounter individuals who are associated with, if not outright members of, what we will ultimately identify as organized crime. Sensing a business opportunity, some of these individuals may just have made more than a few bucks playing with little pieces of paper.

Hopefully, a bigger story will be found here. You will discover how organizations such as the Secret Service and the Postal Inspection Service have changed and evolved over the years. This goes as well for our laws and the judicial system. What may have been acceptable as an investigative technique at the turn of the last century would not make it in today's world. Another discovery was that there is a symbiotic relationship between stamp counterfeiting and those who also counterfeit currency. Where you find one, you frequently find the other.

The chase begins – it is an interesting chase. Let's start with the early days – 1894 to 1940. These are true crime stories that deal with real people.

STAMP COUNTERFEITING

1

Where the Story May Have Begun

Chicago 1895

In the early 1890s, the United States was suffering through one of its periodic economic meltdowns. Chicago had survived the Great Fire and was again being rebuilt into a major metropolis. This was the Gilded Age, and people migrated to the cities to make their fortune. It was considered a failure of character if you could not make yourself rich and powerful through your own efforts. Not surprisingly, this environment would attract not only the hard working, but also its share of charlatans and crooks.

On the local level, law enforcement was mostly dysfunctional. This was especially true where crimes of finesse were involved. Local officials were more concerned with where the next bribe might come from than with upholding the law or protecting the public. Chicago could also claim the distinction of being the home base of Dr. H.H. Holmes, America's first known and one of our most prolific serial killers. On Chicago's south side, Holmes had built his personal palace of secret passages and murder chambers totally on credit and fraud. This had the tacit support of city officials. It is not by accident that to this day Chicago's unofficial motto is "where is mine."

Into this world, on April 4, 1895, Edward Lowry, a Chicago stamp dealer, walked into the office of Captain James E. Stuart of the Bureau of the Post Office Inspectors. After he introduced himself, he innocently asked if the Post Office Department would have any objection to his purchasing postage stamps at less than face value.

Stuart was the agent in charge of the Chicago office and his department was responsible for overseeing the postal operations for the entire Midwest. When his inspectors were not overseeing the operations of the many offices in his jurisdiction, they spent a great deal of time investigating post office burglaries and robberies. When Lowry presented his unusual inquiry, Stuart's interest was immediately piqued.

Lowry explained to Stuart that when he sat down with his Sunday paper an advertisement had caught his eye. On page 16 in the *Chicago Tribune* under the heading "Pictures, Stamps, Coins, etc.," he found the following:

> We have $115 U.S. TWO CENT STAMPS which we cannot use here; will send them by express C.O.D. Privilege of Examination for $100. Canadian Novelty Supply Agency, Hamilton, Ontario, Canada.

Stuart's immediate suspicion was that the stamps in question must have been stolen. Still, he did not know of any recent burglaries or robberies that could be the source of these stamps. This was something that demanded his attention, and Stuart requested that Lowry go forward and place an order. When these items arrived he wanted to get a look at them. Then, Stuart decided to place his own ad. It was scheduled to appear in the next Sunday edition of the same newspaper:

> "Wanted – uncancelled 2-cent postage stamps, address K 188 Tribune office."

Almost immediately there were other developments. Nathan Herzog, who was a local cigar dealer who sold stamps on the side, came on the scene. He had also seen the ad and placed an order for the stamps. On April 8, his package arrived. Being of a suspicious nature, before accepting delivery and paying the C.O.D. charge, he insisted on seeing what he had ordered.

When he opened the parcel, he did not like what he found. The post office issued the regular 2-cent stamp in sheets of 100. The items he found were all in sheets of five stamps by five. When he refused to accept the delivery, the messenger tried to reassure him. He told Herzog these stamps had to be all right as he had already made four other deliveries that very day. Herzog was not moved, and he decided to take his suspicions to the authorities. His first stop was to the deputy U.S. marshal, who directed him to the postal inspectors.

Now, Stuart had something concrete he could work with, and he moved to follow it up. At the Express Office that had tried to deliver the package to Herzog, he identified not only the one for Herzog, but also a number of others. Stuart seized these packages and now with stamps in hand he could begin to figure out what was going on. Stuart had the reputation of being a very capable criminal investigator, but one thing he was not was an expert on stamps. He soon had the assistance of someone who was.

Another individual who had ordered stamps was a Mr. Lefever. This individual was a stamp collector. When his package arrived, Lefever examined them. He noted that these were "peculiar looking 2-cent postage stamps." Knowing that something was not right, and being a good citizen, Lefever took his stamps to the post office. His good deed was promptly rewarded. The government seized his stamps as evidence.

It was either through Lefever or some other person that Captain Stuart was informed there was a local authority he could consult. This was P.M Wolsieffer. In Chicago this individual was an established stamp dealer and auctioneer. To anyone with a question about stamps, he was the person to talk to. This reputation was well deserved. Years later, Wolsieffer would become the president of the American Philatelic Society.

An example of the quandary Stuart found himself facing was later described by Wolsieffer himself. When he walked into Stuart's office he found the agent trying to measure the stamp with a ruler. He introduced the agent to a perforation gauge, and educated him on how it was used. After briefly examining the stamps, Wolsieffer did not hesitate to pronounce them as counterfeit. They were very good copies; he informed Stuart he had no doubt they were counterfeits, and not stolen items.

With the counterfeit nature of the stamps established, Stuart's next step was to contact Captain Porter, who was his friend and counterpart in the Secret Service. Today, when one thinks of the Secret Service, the first thought is that oh, they protect the president. What is frequently forgotten is that the Secret Service was originally created to combat counterfeiting. It was not until 1901 that they were given the additional responsibility for protecting the president. Working together, the two agents began by gathering up other parcels destined for delivery in Chicago.

This activity would not long escape the notice of the press and a few interesting stories began to come out. On April 1, William W. DeWees had sent a telegram to the Canadian address, ordering stamps. For some reason this order was returned as undeliverable. Not being deterred, DeWees then put his order in an envelope, and entrusted it to the post office for delivery. A reply soon came back telling him that his stamps were on the way. He was also informed that if he found that he wished to order more, they could supply him with as many as $300 worth each month.

Another customer whose telegram had also been returned was Archie L. Doherty. When this happened Doherty's response was to just give up. Later interviewed by the press, he made the following observation: "I am glad now I did not get the stamps, for I never would have scrutinized them, as I never yet had occasion to doubt the genuineness of a postage stamp."

DeWees' parcel arrived on April 8 and it contained 23 envelopes, each holding 250 stamps. DeWees gave the messenger a check for $100, counted the stamps, and placed them in his safe. When he opened for business the following morning he found Captain Porter sitting on his doorstep.

He recounted what happened next:

> When Captain Porter's experienced eye fell on them he knew they were spurious. The printing is not so clear as on the genuine. They are said to be lithographs instead of steel engravings. The color is good; the most glaring deficiency is in the size. They are about one-thirty second of an inch larger each way. The paper is good as in the genuine stamp and the gumming on them is much better than of the government's output.

It was inevitable that word would soon slip out and be picked up by the tabloids. On page one of the April 9 editions of the *Chicago Tribune* the news was trumpeted to the world:

POSTAL AUTHORITIES UNEARTH A
STUPENDOUS SWINDLE

Skilled counterfeiters engrave duplicate plates of the two-cent

Stamp of commerce with wonderful accuracy
Capt. Porter and Inspector Stuart seize a package of the
Spurious ones at the Chicago office of the
Wells-Fargo Express Company

Back in the 1890s, the nation's newspapers were not noted for understatement. The story that everyday postage stamps had been counterfeited and were then being found in Chicago was a sensational news story. They immediately identified this event as the most important swindle ever perpetrated on any government. Newspapers across the country did not hesitate to pick up this story and have fun with it.

One newspaper in Nebraska could not resist the opportunity to take their jab at the government. Tongue in cheek, they described one sure way to tell the product of the government from the imitations: "Moisten the gum and place the sample on the upper right hand corner of the envelope. If it sticks, it is a counterfeit."

The public immediately began to speculate as to who could have perpetrated this crime. Some theorized it was the handiwork of disgruntled former employees. Just the preceding July the government had taken over the contract from the private contractors who had previously been printing the government's postage stamps. This was now the responsibility of the U.S. Bureau of Engraving and Printing. The thought was that maybe someone who no longer had a job had, for either profit or spit, started their own printing operation.

To the average person on the street, the bogus stamps would be considered very good copies. When the press questioned Washington Hesing, the Chicago postmaster, he stated he had also seen a sample of these items. His comment was that they were extraordinary. In his opinion, "One million counterfeit stamps such as these could pass through this office every day and not be detected." He described how his post office functioned and how easily copies such as these could slip through the system. "We handle 1,200,000 letters daily, canceling them on machines which have a capacity of 40,000 (pieces) per hour; you can see how it is next to impossible to examine the stamps."

Surprisingly, it was the stamp-collecting community who voiced the strongest doubts about the existence of these counterfeits. For weeks, the philatelic press would question the existence of the bad stamps.[1] They then played down the importance of what this discovery could mean for postal revenue. Collectors of U.S. postage stamps who commonly were themselves defrauded by charlatans apparently could not believe that anyone would actually go to the effort of creating a stamp destined for use in the mail. This is a mindset that unfortunately is shared by the public to this day, and it is also the counterfeiter's greatest defense.

Both Captains Stuart and Porter notified their superiors in Washington about what they were discovering in Chicago. As soon as counterfeit stamps were seized, samples had been dispatched to Washington. When Washington officials had these copies before them, they had no doubts about the danger these stamps posed to postal revenue. The first questions that probably came to mind were just how long these stamps had been in use. The next question was just how widespread had been the distribution. Their fears were fanned when rumors soon circulated that the counterfeiters were operating not only in Chicago, but in Canada, St. Louis, Cincinnati, Buffalo and possibly as far west as San Francisco.

Washington was not slow to act. Chief Hazen of the Secret Service and Chief Inspector Wheeler of the Post Office Department conferred on the problem, and what could be done to address this. Immediately, all across the country, postal inspectors were ordered to check the stamp stock in all large post offices. Then a letter bearing an example of one of the stamps seized in Chicago was dispatched to all postmasters with the following instructions:

POST OFFICE DEPARTMENT
Office of the Third Assistant
Postmaster General

April 10, 1895

Sirs:

     There are in circulation counterfeit two-cent ordinary postage

---

1 Time and again, this would be a common refrain in the stamp - collecting community. The stamp collector and authorities just could not bring themselves to believe that someone would actually do this.

stamps of the Bureau of Engraving and Printing design, as described at the bottom of page 940 of the January 1895, Postal Guide (Triangular ornament in the upper corners and pale carmine tint).

This is one of the spurious stamps {Here was pasted a specimen marked at the upper corner with a letter "C" in ink.}

At the first blush, it has the lighter look of more open engraving, but under the magnifying glass, it will be found that this is attributed to the broken lines – instead of the continuous lines – of the genuine steel engraving. Thus suggesting a recourse to the photo lithographic process in securing the counterfeit resemblance and imprint. These counterfeits are, as far as discovered, well perforated and printed in sheets of five stamps.

You will impart this information at once to your subordinates who handle stamps, and more especially, stamped matter received for transmission and instruct them to scrutinize carefully the stamps thereon, and as far as possible, identify persons mailing any matters with spurious stamps upon them.

The attention of yourself and subordinates will not be confined to the Bureau design but secondarily to the two-cent of 1890 issue which has no ornament in the upper corners.[2]

Upon discovery of important information under these instructions, you will take active measures, and, having by the most expeditious means advised the nearest Post Office Inspector, notify this office.

This letter, with the attached stamp, will be carefully preserved, as you or your successor may be called upon for it.

Very Respectfully,

3rd Ass't P.M. General[3]

Back in Chicago the agents soon concluded that the stamp parcels all seemed to have one common denominator: It appeared they all had originated in Buffalo, New York, and had been transported to Chicago via Wells Fargo & Company. On the night of April 9, Stuart and Porter slipped out of Chicago and began to track

---

2 A special dispatch was found issued on April 9, 1895 from Washington D.C.: "Several weeks ago information came to the Post Office Department that a counterfeit two-cent stamp was being circulated at Boston, Mass., and a sample was sent to the Stamp Division here for examination. It was found to be a clumsily executed photo-lithography, badly blurred." This correspondence presents a mystery. Was this item the product of another unknown counterfeiting operation or possibly the product of an earlier printing of the Chicago fakes? Just throwing this out as food for thought.

3 An interesting point: A number of these stamps so inscribed ultimately found their way out of postal filing cabinets and on to the stamp market to be sold as collector's items.

the stamps back to their point of origin. Their first stop was Buffalo where at the Wells Fargo office they were told the suspected parcels had all been brought into their office by a woman. They remembered that she had made a number of visits, and each time would pull a number of prepackaged parcels out of a satchel she had used to transport them.

Gathering all the information they could from Wells Fargo, the next stop on their journey was Hamilton, Ontario, Canada. Going to the address that had appeared in the newspaper advertisement, the agents demonstrated better luck finding the address than the Western Union messenger had. It was located just down the block from the municipal police department. At No. 22 King William Street the outside sign identified the business as a printers and glaziers shop. When they questioned Arther Fish, the proprietor, they found that he had rented desk space to a Mr. George Morrison, who was conducting business under the name of the Novelty and Supply Agency.

The agents could not locate Morrison, but they did find another person in attendance. Working at a desk was a woman who when questioned identified herself as Mary T. Mack. She stated she had been just recently engaged by Morrison to work as his clerk. She told the agents that at the moment she really had no idea where her employer could be found. Her story was that the day after she had been hired, Morrison had left, saying he was going to Toronto to open another office.

She stated she expected Morrison to return any day, but for now she was receiving all of her instructions by mail. As for the stamps she was shipping, her story was that Morrison had told her that he sometimes received stamps in lieu of cash for merchandise sold to customers in the United States. These stamps could not be used in Canada, so he was reselling them at a discount to customers south of the border.

The agents did not believe this story for a minute, but it was decided that at this time the woman would not be arrested. While the agents continued their investigation, the Canadian authorities agreed to restrict her freedom of movement and to keep tabs on her activities. Searching in Hamilton for any trace of the missing Mr. Morrison, the agents found someone using that name had stayed at the St. Nicholas

Hotel. He had checked in on April 1, the day after the ad had appeared in the *Chicago Tribune*, but now was gone. Exhausting the leads in Canada, and now armed with Morrison's description, Stuart and Porter returned to Chicago.

In their absence from Chicago the local investigation had continued. On April 11, one of Porter's agents had received information from a citizen about suspicious activities. Mr. C. H. Felton was not sure exactly what was going on, but he reported that day after day he heard what he suspected was the pounding of a printing press from the apartment over his head. Then there were what he considered to be "suspicious" individuals continually coming and going to that apartment at all hours of the day and night.

Secret Service Agent Daniel White went to 26 Carl Street to find out what might be going on. He found the second floor was rented to a Mrs. Lacy and her daughter, Tinsey McMillan. Searching the flat (without a warrant) he found a locked back room. When he forced this door open he discovered a perforating machine, blank copper plates, etching inks, gummed paper, and a camera. The information was correct. This was a den of criminal activity.

Professing her innocence, Mrs. Lacy denied being involved in any criminal activity by either herself or her daughter. She explained that the printing equipment was the private property of her daughter who was simply doing some work for a downtown firm. She was sorry, but no, the agent could not talk to her. She had left town for Denver two weeks ago, and she really had no idea when she would be returning.

Continuing the investigation, Agent White discovered there had been two frequent visitors to 26 Carl St. The names they had given were "Mr. Jones" and "Mr. Cushing." With descriptions of these individuals, the agent took up a surveillance of the apartment, and when Captain Porter returned gave him a full report on what he had been up to in his absence.

Porter then told Agent White about his trip to Buffalo and Hamilton. Comparing notes, they soon concluded the woman in Canada matched that of a portrait Mrs. Lacy had of her daughter. Then, Porter pulled another rabbit out of his hat. He informed White that he had recognized the woman in Canada as someone with whom he was already acquainted.

Four years earlier a woman from Chicago, who was using the name of Tese McMillan, had hired an informant used by the Secret Service to teach her how to make plaster molds to produce counterfeit silver coins. Not wishing to burn his informant and maybe be forced to put him in jail for assisting in the commission of a crime, Porter had stopped this enterprise before a criminal offense had actually been committed.[4]

As difficult as it was in the 1890s, Porter began to dig into the background of Mrs. Lacy's daughter. It seemed that her real name was Mary Tinsey McMillan. In addition to her adventure in coin counterfeiting, it became fairly evident they were dealing with an established criminal. In St. Louis she had purchased furniture on credit. After shipping the items to Chicago for resale, she had skipped out on the bill. In Chicago, she had defrauded an insurance company out of $1,100. Porter suspected the case he was now dealing with involved more than just a newspaper ad and a few shipments of counterfeit stamps.

During Captain Stuart's absence, the local inspector's office had also been developing some interesting information. The circular that Washington D.C. had sent out was beginning to show results. On April 16, the Kansas City Post Office notified their local inspectors that items bearing the counterfeit stamps and postmarked from Chicago were being identified in the Kansas City mail. The mailer was identified as one Warren T. Thomson, the owner and editor of a matrimonial newspaper called *Heart and Hand*. This was another person the authorities knew well. Only the month before, both Thomson and his newspaper had been convicted by the postal inspectors of mail fraud.

When Porter received this information from Stuart, he took two of his agents and went to 69 Dearborn Street, the newspaper's address. When they arrived, Thomson was not there. This did not deter Porter. He began to search the office and when he found that it had a safe, he forced it open. No counterfeits were found in either the

---

4 Porter is showing surprising restraint. It is common for either agents or their informants to set up or even carry out counterfeit production. Good counterfeiting is not easy, and individuals with this skill are in high demand. In one case I had to provide the perforations for a sample of counterfeit stamps. I had the Bureau of Engraving do the work for me. My partners were impressed with the results.

office or the safe.

It was about this time that Thomson walked in and demanded to know what was going on. This did not faze Porter for a moment, and he soon took control and started to ask his own questions. Most likely it was like two dogs confronting each other and Thomson soon found that he was the one backing down. In response to Porter's interrogation, Thomson acknowledged that, yes, he had been using the stamps in question. The story he gave was that he had responded to an ad he had found in the newspaper and innocently purchased $225 worth of the discounted items. He was sorry, but no, he could not surrender any of these stamps to the agent for his examination. They had already been used up in his mailings. Oh, and of course, he had no idea they were counterfeit stamps when he purchased and used them.

Porter decided that Thomson and his story had to be looked into just a little bit further. He was asked to accompany the agent back to his office to clear up a few more points. Early on, Porter and Stuart had decided that individuals who innocently purchased and used these stamps would not be charged. When Porter conferred with Stuart about Thomson it was decided that an exception just might be made in this case. For his part, Stuart did not believe the story Thomson was spinning for a minute. He knew this man, and in Stuart's view, he was a criminal. Even though there was no evidence against him, it was decided they would still hold him in custody.[5]

This was not a shot in the dark. Besides Thomson's sterling character, when Porter had been taking Thomson's office apart, it had not escaped his notice that Thomson had an employee named Charles O. Jones. This person just happened to also match the description of the mysterious George Morrison, the reported owner of the Canadian Novelty Supply Agency. It was also noted with interest that Jones had worked for several years at various Chicago newspapers.

In 1895, newspapers were frequently illustrated not with photographs, but with etchings. Porter determined this was a skill at which Jones was proficient. It also happened to be the skill that was needed for the production of counterfeit printing plates. When the agents identified Jones as being one of the visitors to 26 Carl Street,

---

5 Chicago cops over the years would have a description for this. The charge is aggravated mopery.

McMillan's address, and the location of the printing press, it was decided to pull him in as well.

The arrest took place on the night of April 17. Stuart, Porter and a deputy U.S. Marshal went to the residence of Charles O. Jones, where he resided with his wife and father-in-law. He was upstairs when the officers arrived, and when he came down in answer to their summons, he was informed they had a warrant for his arrest. Witnessing the arrest, his wife was immediately reduced to hysterics. She and her father implored the officers to release their prisoner, arguing that he could not have been involved in any criminal activity.

Somehow the newspapers had also gotten word that this arrest was about to occur. The reporters were right behind the officers, and when they left with their prisoner, reporters rushed in to interview his wife. She denied her husband was one of the counterfeiters, and then went on to say, "The story that my husband had made frequent trips to Montreal, or even Buffalo, is absolutely without foundation. He has not been out of the city recently, with the exception of a short trip to Kansas City."

Neither Stuart nor Porter was moved by the family's pleas. They had marched Charles Jones off in irons. Then, from 9 p.m. until after 2 the next morning he was grilled by the agents. Still, he would not be moved off his story. He was still professing his innocence early the next morning when the agents finally left him alone in his cell to ponder his fate.

On April 19, Jones was taken before United States Commissioner Humphry where he was formally charged with making counterfeit postage stamps. Secret Service Agent Daniel White was the first witness the government called. He related the story of his search of the 26 Carl Street address where Tinsey McMillan resided with her mother. White described how he had searched the flat and subsequently entered the locked back room. He testified that in the room he had found a printing press and other printing paraphernalia. Then Assistant United States Attorney Rosenthal asked a significant question, "Did you find anything there besides the tools?"

Dramatically, White then drew an envelope out of his pocket and pulled out a strip of perforated paper. He explained how he had found the scrap among some burnt papers in the dining room stove. The agent further explained how the perforations on this scrap of paper matched those on the counterfeit stamps. "And here is something else," said the officer. He then brought out a single counterfeit stamp and announced, "I also found this in the house."

Nathan Herzog, the cigar dealer from the Chicago Chamber of Commerce Building, was called to testify. He related how he had seen the advertisement in the *Chicago Tribune* offering to sell discounted postage, and how he had responded to it. He was then shown a package of counterfeit stamps. He identified this package as the one that had been delivered to him by the messenger on April 8, and which he had refused to accept.

With the testimony of Agent White, the counterfeit nature of the stamps was established, and they were tied to 26 Carl Street. Herzog's testimony established the stamps were then shipped from the Canadian Novelty Supply Agency. The next witnesses would tie Charles Jones directly to this establishment in Canada.

George Smith, who was the proprietor of the St. Nicholas Hotel in Hamilton, Ontario, was called. He identified Jones as the man who used the name of George Morrison when he registered at his hotel. Arther Fish then identified Jones as the man who rented a desk at 22 King William Street to conduct his business. Jones had again used the name of George Morrison and identified his enterprise as the Canadian Novelty Supply Agency. In addition to identifying Jones as Morrison, both witnesses related how they believed the accused had attempted to use a disguise. In Canada he had been wearing eyeglasses and he had sported a small mustache.

Jones' attorney, L.B. Hillas, argued his client should be released and the charges dismissed. His contention was that the government had failed to connect his client with the stamps that were identified as being counterfeit. This was a preliminary hearing, and not a trial, and all that the prosecution needed to do was show probable cause. Still, I would contend that his attorney was attacking the wrong part of the government's case. In the records of the hearing, it did not seem that a firm establishment was made that the stamps in question were actually counterfeit. Then again, this was a case being presented by the Secret Service and the postal inspectors. When a court official at a preliminary hearing is told an item is counterfeit, that is all that is needed.

Commissioner Humphry did not buy the argument that had been put forward by Jones' attorney. He found the government had amply established "probable cause" to believe Jones was a part of this criminal scheme. He remanded Jones to the custody of the U.S. Marshal pending a trial, and a bond of $5,000 was set. Now the government had to go on and build the cases on the other suspects.

Believing that Jones was now safely in jail, the two agents returned to Canada. There, working with the Canadian authorities, Mary T. Mack was officially identified as Tinsey McMillan, an American citizen who actually resided in Chicago. The Canadian authorities agreed to take her into custody pending her extradition back to the United States. The question of this extradition actually presented an interesting legal question. Under the existing treaties in 1895, it was debatable if the counterfeiting of postage stamps was an extraditable offense. Mrs. McMillan immediately hired an attorney to fight any attempt to remove her to the United States.

The government considered this a groundbreaking case. As such, Chief Hazen, the director of the Secret Service, took personal command of the extradition procedure. He requested and then received the papers from President Grover Cleveland for the arrest and removal of Tinsey McMillan. Filing them with the Canadian authorities, he then took care to wait the required 15 days. This time delay is built into the system to give a defense attorney an opportunity to file an appeal in any U.S. District Court to fight an extradition.

Actually, McMillan's attorney had another idea. Rather than go into a United States court, he went to Toronto and received a writ of habeas corpus to block her removal. If he could serve these papers on Chief Hazen, a delay of at least three months would result while the issue was argued in Canada.

When Hazen discovered what was occurring, he had to devise a way to avoid being served. Some Canadian officials became co-conspirators with him and assisted in his mission. Before McMillan's attorney could find out he was in the country, with no fan fair Hazen slipped into Canada, and then into the prison where McMillan was being held. Discovering McMillan was about to be moved, her attorney rushed to the prison in an attempt to intercept the agent. There he was stonewalled by the authorities who would not let him serve his papers. With too many doors to watch, the attorney rushed off to the train station figuring he would intercept Hazen and his prisoner there.

Again Hazen was one step ahead of him. Instead of the station, with his prisoner in tow, he took a coach eight miles out of town to a place called Stony Creek. The only structure there was a telegraph office, and Hazen used the wire to contact the superintendent of the railroad. An express train was ordered to stop and pick up their unusual passengers. Back in Hamilton while McMillan's attorney was pacing the train platform, Hazen and his prisoner were being whisked to the United States.

Hazen was still not home free. He suspected another attempt to intercept him might be made when they got to the border. To counter any such attempt, just before the train reached the international suspension bridge, he moved his prisoner to a stateroom at the front of the train. When the train was stopped for customs, if the habeas corpus papers had been there, they could not be served. The Pullman car containing the officer and his prisoner were now sitting on the U.S. side of the border. Tinsey McMillan may have been furious, but she was also officially a prisoner in the United States.

Charges against Mary T. McMillan were filed in Buffalo, and on June 5 she appeared before the United States commissioner. According to one newspaper account the government had a surprise waiting for her. At the beginning of the case, Stuart and Porter had learned that the woman bringing the parcels of stamps to Wells Fargo had always transported them in a distinctive satchel. This was an identifiable piece of evidence, and unbeknownst to McMillan, this satchel had been found.

Following the government agents' first visit to Canada, McMillan's freedom of movement had been severely restricted. She had not been in jail, but she was under continual surveillance. Knowing that the law was closing in, she desperately was trying to dispose of any incriminating evidence she had in her possession. Before this could be accomplished, she saw the officers approaching, and in a panic had left the satchel on the terrace of the building where she was staying.

The agents had never informed her that it subsequently had

been recovered and identified as her property. In court, it was presented as evidence along with the reported $28,000 in counterfeit postage stamps found inside. The press reported that it was at this point in the proceedings she fainted.

On September 19, the government's case was presented to a federal grand jury. Not surprisingly, a true bill was shortly returned which indicted Mary T. (Tinsey) McMillan, aka Mary T. Mack, on the following counts:

Count One – On April 5, 1895, Mary T. McMillan did knowingly, wrongfully, unlawfully, feloniously, falsely make, forge and counterfeit certain postage stamps of the United States of America. To wit, thirty-eight thousand postage stamps of a denomination and value of two-cents.

Count Two – On April 5, 1895, Mary T. McMillan did knowingly, wrongfully and unlawfully, feloniously utter and publish as true, use and sell 5,750 forged and counterfeited postage stamps.

Count Three – On April 5, 1895, Mary T. McMillan did knowingly, wrongfully and unlawfully, feloniously utter and publish as true, and sell 5,750 forged and counterfeited postage stamps.

Count Four – Certain persons whose names are to the jurors unknown did knowingly, wrongfully and unlawfully, falsely make, and print forged and counterfeit (here is pasted a counterfeit stamp) thirty eight thousand postage stamps each of which said postage stamps was then and there of the denomination of two cents (here is pasted a counterfeit stamp). Mary T. McMillan on the fifth day of April did utter and publish as true and deliver five thousand seven hundred and fifty said stamps to William T. DeWees.

Count Five – Certain persons whose names are to the jurors unknown, did knowingly, wrongfully and unlawfully, falsely make, print, forge and counterfeit 38,000 postage stamps. Mary T. McMillan at Buffalo, New York on the 5th day of April 1895 with the intent to defraud the postal revenue of the United States did after the same were printed, utter and publish as true and deliver 28,750 of said false, forged and counterfeited postage stamps to Wells Fargo and Company Express.

Having successfully indicted Mary McMillan, and having her safely in jail, the agents returned to Chicago. What they discovered was that in their absence Jones had been released on $5,000 bail. When Jones saw the newspaper accounts of McMillan's arrest and indictment, he knew his own number would soon be up. Instead of waiting for his world to collapse, he fled the city.

Not only did Jones flee the city, he left the state. In the criminal justice world of 1895, this should have given him a free pass. Very seldom were criminals chased from one jurisdiction to another. Unfortunately for Jones, he was not dealing with local law enforcement. Federal agents do not recognize geographic boundaries, and he really should have recognized that after their counterfeiting operation had been traced to Canada and broken up.

Once he felt safe in another location, he sent several letters to the Secret Service trying to cut a deal. Intimating that if the government would only agree to dismiss the charges against him, he could turn over the plates used to produce the stamps. When this correspondence was brought to the attention of Chief Hazen, the chief had other ideas. As far as he was concerned, there would be no deals with this fugitive. Jones' letters had been posted from Cincinnati, Ohio, and Hazen directed Porter to go there and take Jones back into custody.

This was not exactly like looking for a needle in a haystack. Porter knew that Jones' parents lived in Cincinnati, and in correspondence the agent routed through them, it was hinted that some agreement might be possible. Jones was lured into a meeting. Not surprisingly, after his interrogation by Porter and Stuart, these were two individuals he did not wish to see again. When he saw Porter approaching, Jones tried to run. On November 2, he found himself in chains as Porter's prisoner and on his way back to Chicago. When forced to recognize the seriousness of the situation, he was now ready to talk to the authorities.[6]

It appears Jones must have been very forthcoming. Warren T. Thomson had also been released on bail, but now on November 9,

---

6 There is an important lesson to learn here. It is perfectly legal for an agent to lie or misrepresent something in the interrogation or negotiations with a subject in a criminal case. If you don't have it in writing and before your attorney, it does not mean a thing. What you say or do can be used against you.

Postal Inspector Christian was dispatched to take Thomson again into custody. While this was occurring, Agent Porter and Inspector Stuart went to the Masonic Temple. This time they had a search warrant and it gave them access to the safety deposit vault. Inside they hit pay dirt.

Apparently in April after Jones and Thomson had been released on bail, they had gathered all of their counterfeiting paraphernalia and had them in the Masonic Temple. When the agents went into the vault, they discovered a box identified as the property of their suspects. Inside they found 130 copper printing plates and an additional 30,000 counterfeit postage stamps.

Again arrested, Thomson was marched back into federal court where he received a chilly reception. As Thomson had not violated his bond the first time, the judge again set a bond of $5,000. Thomson again went to Charles A. Fuller, the bondsman who had originally posted security for him, but this time he was turned down. Thus, unable to post his bail bond, the U.S. Marshals provided him with lodgings in the Joliet federal prison until his trial.

Porter still did not consider this investigation over. As a Secret Service agent his primary job was investigating counterfeit currency, and he demonstrated a mindset common in Secret Service agents to this day. He reasoned that if someone is going to counterfeit stamps, at some point they are going to try their hand at making their own money as well. Adding fuel to this suspicion was the fact that the newly cooperative Jones had been dropping hints along those same lines.

Porter had never been impressed with the veracity of Mrs. Lacy, Mary McMillan's mother, and he decided to lean on her a bit more. He swore out a search warrant for the new residence where Mrs. Lacy had relocated. This search produced virtually no results, but that had not been unexpected. Porter's whole idea was to rattle her cage, and run a bluff.

When he left Lacy's residence, his next stop was with her attorney, C.W. Monroe. He gave Monroe an ultimatum: Produce the plates for making the money or both Monroe and his client just might become guests of the government. At the very least he promised to make both of their lives miserable for however long it was in his power to do so.[7]

Porter should have been a poker player. His bet paid off. The next day, a messenger delivered a package to Deputy U.S. Marshal Van Prang. Inside the package the deputy found printing plates to produce $10 U.S. bank notes of the Series 1891. There also was a note: "Here is a package Mrs. Lacy wished me to hand to you or Captain Porter. Mrs. Lacy has an affidavit setting forth where she got it and that it is the only suspicious article she had in her possession or ever had. I hope this will be satisfactory. C.W. Monroe, Attorney for Mrs. Lacy."

One might conclude the newspaper reporters had a listening device in Captain Porter's office. They learned of the existence of the counterfeit plates to produce currency about as fast as Porter did. The immediate assumption was that Thomson, the last person arrested, must have been the source of the story.

It then turned out that C.W. Monroe represented not only Mrs. Lacy but also Warren Thomson, and he was talking to the press. He vehemently denied that either of his clients were responsible, or had anything to do with counterfeit money. He put the responsibility for the plates to produce currency squarely on the shoulders of Charles Jones:

> Jones left the plates with Mrs. Lacy. The day the Secret Service
> Officers traced the making of the counterfeit stamps to Mrs. Lacy's flat
> on Carl Street, Jones called at the flat. He handed the plates done up in a
> package to Mrs. Lacy. He asked her to take charge of them. Before he could
> explain the matter, one of the Secret Service men entered the flat, and
> Jones left by the rear door. The Secret Service Agent [Daniel White] sat
> talking to Mrs. Lacy for an hour, with his elbow resting on the package on
> the table.

When Porter made his demand on Mrs. Lacy and subsequently her attorney, it is not surprising that the threats he made would be taken very seriously. Both Captain Porter and Inspector Stuart were well-known commodities on the Chicago scene. Their exploits were frequently reported in the press. In the preceding six-month period alone, Stuart had been involved in two separate shooting incidents. When these men had someone in their sights, their targets could

---

7 Something to note here: When you make a Secret Service agent angry, do not expect him or her to play nice. It is not in their gene pool.

expect immediate or eventual incarceration. These were not men to trifle with, or lightly defy.

On November 18, 1895, Mrs. Lacy's daughter, Mary T. McMillan, went on trial in Auburn, New York. Appearing as witnesses were the Chicago tobacco dealer Nathan Herzog, and Edward Massouth, a Chicago stamp dealer. Both men testified they had ordered stamps but had refused to accept them when they examined them and concluded they were counterfeit. Thomas J. Sullivan, the assistant chief of the Bureau of Engraving and Printing, testified as to the counterfeit nature of the stamps. Representatives of the Wells Fargo Express Company identified Mary McMillan as the person who gave them various packages for delivery. They testified that the identified parcels that contained the counterfeit stamps had been dispatched by them for delivery in Chicago.

Both Captain Porter of the Secret Service and Captain Stuart of the Inspection Service were used to lay out the government's case, their investigation, and the discoveries they had made. Reflecting on the importance of this case in the mind of the government, the entire proceeding was witnessed by William P. Hazen, chief of the Secret Service. Not surprisingly, on November 21, the jury found Mary T. McMillan guilty on all counts, and U.S. District Judge Alfred Coke sentenced her to one year and six months in jail, to be served in the Erie County Penitentiary.

Now the Chicago end of the case needed to be tied up. Philip Bulfer had posted property and $3,000 cash as bond for the release of Charles Jones. On June 2, 1897, a handwritten indictment was filed by the U.S. Attorney John C. Black charging Jones with four counts:

1. Forging and counterfeiting 77,250 stamps in the likeness of the two-cent postage stamp.

2. That he possessed with intent to use and sell 11,250 forged and counterfeited postage stamps in the likeness of the 2-cent postage stamp.

3. That he sold to Warren T. Thomson 11,250 forged and counterfeited postage stamps in the likeness of the 2-cent postage stamp.

4. That Jones forged and counterfeited ten dies and ten plates and engravings, each in the likeness of the 2-cent postage stamp.

These were serious charges, and at least on paper, Jones could have been looking at 20 to 40 years in prison. After his second arrest he had concluded that it was time to play let's make a deal. In return for his cooperation, information provided, and subsequent testimony against Thomson, the prosecutor agreed that he would only be sentenced to serve 10 months in jail. Special Agent Daniel White, the agent who had been held up for ridicule in the news stories that told of his using the counterfeit currency plates as an armrest, was given the assignment of transporting this prisoner to his new lodgings in the Joliet prison.

Thomson's indictment was filed on October 15, 1895. It only charged him with possession with the intent to use 11,200 counterfeit stamps that had been supplied to him by Jones. This indictment had been prepared before the agents made the seizure of counterfeit plates from the vault of the Masonic Temple. On May 11, 1897, two years and one month after the chase began, Thomson was convicted on this charge, and sentenced to one year in prison.

All things considered, Warren Thomson got off easy. Every indication is that he may have been the original mastermind behind this scheme. If so, for his day he did come up with an original idea. Running his mail-dependent business, a large part of his expense was the cost incurred in both advertising and mailing his product – his matrimonial newspaper. It is my suspicion that Warren Thomson contracted for the production of counterfeit stamps he could use to conduct this business.

Reaching this momentous decision, the fact that he had a skilled engraver already in his employ would have made his effort so much easier. It was only reasonable that the person he would turn to for advice and assistance would have been Charles Jones. The records show that when the plan was put into action it was Thomson who purchased a 10-inch Rosback perforating machine from Mr. S. M. Wetherby. Then, at Thomson's direction, this machine was to be delivered to Charles Jones. It can be speculated that Jones facilitated the introduction of Thomson to Mary McMillan.

It is not really known if Thomson had anything to do with the distribution of the stamps from Canada. A reasonable surmise is that after Jones and Mary McMillan had produced the original printing for Thomson, the pair just may have decided that this was too good of a deal to just let go. Quite possibly, Thomson was just as surprised as Postal Inspector Stuart was when the bogus stamps were offered for sale to the general public.

How big was this scheme? As this information was never shared with the public nobody really knows. In the *Annual Report of the Fourth Assistant Postmaster General* for 1895, he stated that fewer than 100,000 of the stamps were produced. Very possibly this was correct, but it is also possible this was wishful thinking on the part of the Post Office Department.

Almost, if not all of the 100,000 figure given for this bogus stamp printing were accounted for in the arrests and seizures made in Chicago and Hamilton, Canada. No official mention has been found relating to the counterfeit 2-cent 1894 stamps distributed to other cities. Evidence exists that this distribution did occur. One postal cover bearing this bogus stamp exists with an April 2, 1895 Kansas City postmark. Another item bears two counterfeit stamps and is postmarked November 9, 1897 from Portland, Oregon.

Giving further evidence that distribution extended to the West Coast, there was a second envelope also mailed in Portland, Oregon. This one was dated July 5, 1901.

Of interest to those who collect stamps, almost immediately with the discovery of this stamp, the question arose as to the legality of a private citizen or organization possessing counterfeit stamps. Since the 1895 case, it has been the official position of the Treasury Department that the possession of counterfeit stamps is illegal. This is a policy that may work with counterfeit currency, but not with counterfeit stamps. The only thing this policy has accomplished is to drive public knowledge of counterfeits (and the trade in them) underground.

Segments of the stamp-collecting public have never agreed with or observed the prohibition against possessing/collecting counterfeit stamps. Many collectors consider counterfeits highly desirable items. In the July 4, 1903 issue of *Mekeel's Weekly Stamp News*, the following story was related:

> That celebrated philatelist, now deceased, Washington Hesing when postmaster of Chicago, in the course of his remarks at a banquet of stamp collectors, shortly after the discovery of the counterfeit 2c stamps, United States, said that the possession of a specimen of one of the forgeries would render the holder liable to arrest. After hearing that statement collectors who were indifferent previously about securing one of the forgeries lost all apathy and became particularly anxious to obtain a specimen of the counterfeit. The result was that the forgeries were treasured, and one had to give large value in good stamps for the blacklisted variety.

Despite his stated position, it is interesting to note that Postmaster Hesing, within days of the counterfeits' discovery, had in his possession a block of 10 of the stamps. In addition, an interesting footnote to the possession angle was found in the *American Journal of Philately* of May 1, 1895.

The editor was able to present a detailed article on the counterfeit stamps because: "Mr. Alfred L. Holman, through the courtesy of Mr. Hesing, the Postmaster at Chicago, has kindly sent us for inspection a block of ten of the famous counterfeit 2-cent stamps." Then there were comments by Elmer Stuart in *Linn's Weekly Stamp News*, November 9, 1935: "At that time not much interest was shown in these counterfeits by collectors; however, some copies were obtained by them. Dr. Cottlow (a possible friend of Hesing) received three copies from the Hon. Washington Hesing, then Postmaster of Chicago." It would seem that Mr. Hesing's instincts as a stamp collector sometimes prevailed over what the Treasury Department might conclude were his obligations as a postmaster. Philatelic items falling through the cracks of the government's prohibition were not limited to Mr. Hesing.

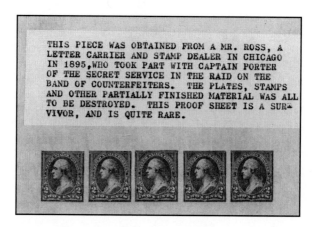

THIS PIECE WAS OBTAINED FROM A MR. ROSS, A LETTER CARRIER AND STAMP DEALER IN CHICAGO IN 1895, WHO TOOK PART WITH CAPTAIN PORTER OF THE SECRET SERVICE IN THE RAID ON THE BAND OF COUNTERFEITERS. THE PLATES, STAMPS AND OTHER PARTIALLY FINISHED MATERIAL WAS ALL TO BE DESTROYED. THIS PROOF SHEET IS A SURVIVOR, AND IS QUITE RARE.

A number of philatelic articles have been found describing copies of the 1895 bogus stamp with the letter "C" (designating counterfeit) written on the stamp. These stamps appeared in various philatelic auctions. Remember the warning notices sent out to postmasters. Obviously someone in Washington forgot to ever call them back. It should not be a surprise that a number of these items would find their way into the hands of private collectors.

It has been argued that the government's decision to put a watermark on new stamp issues was a direct result of this Chicago counterfeit case. Most likely that was not the case, because there simply was not enough lead time between the discovery of the counterfeit and the issuing of new stamps printed on watermarked paper. Once it was brought back, that particular security device would be utilized on U.S. stamps until 1917.

TECHNICAL DETAILS OF THE 1895 CHICAGO COUNTERFEIT

Probable stamp being duplicated: U.S. #250, Type I

It is believed that this stamp was printed between December 1894 and March 1895 in Chicago, Illinois. Known distribution occurred from Hamilton, Ontario, Canada, via Wells Fargo Express Company in Buffalo, New York. It is known that these items were distributed and used in Chicago, Denver, Kansas City and the West Coast area.

These counterfeit stamps were printed from copper electrotype plates in panes of five by five (25 stamps), five by three (15 stamps), and in strips of five. The stamps were printed on thin, coarsely woven white paper. The stamp size ranged from 19-19.5 X 22.5-23 mm. The gum is smooth and of a light yellow color. The upper-corner triangles are those of #250, Type I.

This counterfeit is a lithographed stamp. The background of the central oval is poorly done; more than half of it is solid. The color is a good rendering of the true rose-carmine color of the genuine stamp. The stamps were perforated on a 10-inch Rosback perforating machine. Both the genuine and counterfeit are perforation 12. Using the right side (decimal notation) of a Stanley Gibson Instanta perforation gauge, the genuine stamp measures 12.07. The perforation on the counterfeit measures 11.80.

ADDENDUM

Psst ... Ya wanna buy a counterfeit?

There is a well-established legal mindset that it is "illegal" to own counterfeit stamps. The Secret Service goes out of its way to enforce this view, sometimes to ridiculous extremes. The end result of this approach has generally been counterproductive to the interests of the government. It has made both the discovery and the investigation of counterfeit stamp cases much more difficult. It has been the stamp collector who frequently discovers the existence of these items. What motivation is there to report your discovery if you knew that the government was going to swoop in and take your new treasure from you? If there is an up side to this, it is that the prohibition itself has created collector demand.

Postal counterfeits do have a market. Inadvertently, this has created another "business opportunity" for the unscrupulous. When a counterfeit sells for more than the legitimate item, there is a potential for fraud. It is inevitable that con men would take advantage of this situation. There have been counterfeits of counterfeits – these are aimed at the collector.

An instructive story about the counterfeiting of a counterfeit was related by Harry Weiss in the January 6, 1951, issue of *Weekly Philatelic Gossip*. He reprinted a column originally penned by Michael MacDougall of the McClure Syndicate.

> If someone tried to sell you a counterfeit two-cent stamp for $10 you'd probably think him crazy as well as crooked. That is, you would if you weren't a stamp collector. For only in the curious world of philately is such a strange financial transaction possible. And, as cliché mongers say, therein hangs a tale.
>
> Back in 1894, a Chicago forger marketed untold numbers of phony two-cent stamps, thousands of which did postal duty. It was an exceedingly clever imitation. The color was okay, the perforations matched, the design was perfect. However, there were minute differences. The genuine stamp was on soft paper, the counterfeit on hard; the original measured 19X22 millimeters, the copy 21X24.

Perhaps the fraud never would have been discovered if the ordinary two-cent stamps of 1894 hadn't been issued in three different types. To the inexperienced eye they all looked alike, but stamp enthusiasts could easily spot the variations in design. Type I was much rarer than Type II and III, and philatelists were always on the lookout for it. Unfortunately for the counterfeiter, his private reproductions were all of the scarce Type I variety.

Alert collectors noticed the sudden increase in these hitherto seldom-seen stamps; noticed too the slight differences in paper and size. Postal Inspectors were notified, and the hunt was on. Eventually they crashed in on the counterfeiter and, after a struggle, put him in handcuffs.[8]

After the trial the stock of fraudulent stamps were burned, the plates destroyed. And the government took further steps to prevent a repetition of the crime. Up till then all postage stamps had been printed on unwatermarked paper. In 1895 the then current series was re-issued on paper watermarked U.S.P.S. [sic – the watermark stands for "United States Postage Stamp"]. As far as the authorities were concerned the case was closed. Not so for philatelists. For them the episode was just beginning. Immediately there was a feverish search for letters franked with the phony stamp. Although many thousands must have passed through the mails, less than a hundred were recovered. Prices rose accordingly. Covers with the genuine stamp could be bought anywhere for a few cents; those with the fake brought $5 or more.

Why the mad scramble? Ordinary collectors wanted an interesting addition to their albums; specialists needed the counterfeit for their referenced libraries; non-collectors considered it an unusual oddity. Whatever the reasons, interests never died. Time passed, the price rose constantly. Last year stamp dealers, when they had the "Chicago counterfeit" in stock, asked a minimum of $20. Then the government re-entered the case. The powers-that-be decided to enforce the law prohibiting the possession of any counterfeit stamp, used or unused. Some dealers surrendered their stock of facsimiles. A few hid them.

All reputable auction houses refused to handle the questionable merchandise. Anyone desiring to dispose of a phony stamp now has to do so with a wink and a whisper.

As always, under such conditions, the sharpshooters moved in. I recently witnessed a rather clever swindle with an absolutely original twist. I, too, am a paper chaser, hence familiar with the facts outlined. So I wasn't

---

8 This is a great illustration of how history can be rewritten, and inaccuracies pasted into folklore.

too surprised when, while attending a stamp auction, the stranger on my right handed me a cover and asked if I knew what it was. The letter was postmarked Chicago, July 14, 1894. "Could be the Chicago counterfeit," I hesitated, "It is," said the stranger, "and it's for sale. You can have it for ten bucks." I shook my head, and handed the cover back. But the peddler wasn't so easily discouraged. He produced a millimeter gauge.

"Measure the stamp," he urged. "It's the real thing. You see it's larger than normal."

"I don't doubt it." I replied, "But I have no use for it. I collect mint stamps, not covers."

Obviously disappointed, he pocketed his treasure, moved to another seat. I again centered my attention on the auctioneer.

When the sale was over, I started to leave. At the entrance a happy collector was showing a new acquisition to some friends. I joined the group. It was the same cover I'd been offered an hour before. Why was the owner so eager to get rid of it? I wondered. A little patience and he could have gotten $20 instead of ten. Such a bargain, secured from a total stranger, is always suspect. I asked if I might examine the letter. The stamp had a washed-out appearance, but even so, the printing looked too sharp for lithography. I studied the design, and the telltale mark practically leaped out at me. "Did you measure this stamp?" I asked.

"Sure did," said the collector. "It's the right size."

"Maybe so, but just the same you've been stung. This isn't a counterfeit; it's a counterfeit of a counterfeit. The stamp has been removed, soaked in water, stretched and replaced."

The collector retrieved his purchase, examined it carefully. "Looks all right to me," he said. "How can you tell?"

"All the phony stamps were Type I," I explained. "This one is Type III." The dejected buyer looked again and nodded. Then he dashed out of the room, obviously on the trail of the swindler. Whether or not he caught the gyp artist I don't know. But suppose he did? What could he do? I know it's illegal to sell a counterfeit stamp as genuine, but is it unlawful to sell a genuine stamp as counterfeit?

Again, Michael MacDougall may have had some difficulties with the details of the original case, but nothing is wrong with the dramatic storytelling of his experience. Even in 1951, it is obvious that the 1895 bogus stamp was still of interest to the philatelic world. A con man was able to take advantage of that interest and use it to his advantage. This time the 1895 counterfeit defrauded a collector, instead of the government.

I had encountered counterfeit stamps in my own childhood collection, but it is only fitting that my interest in researching counterfeits began with the 1895 stamp. One day a local Chicago stamp dealer who knew I investigated counterfeiting took me aside – "Psst ... ya wanna see the first counterfeit?"

Was the 1895 case really the first time stamps were used to defraud the United States Postal Revenue? I'm not so sure. When I was digging through old postal records I found a letter that referred to the existence of a counterfeit found in Boston. The Inspection Service has always been notoriously reticent of letting the public know what they are doing. That is why they were given the nickname the "Silent Service." Aggravating this situation is their propensity to archive away and then lose or destroy old case files – "THERE IS NO OFFICIAL HISTORICAL RECORD."

When researching old stamp cases the best source for referrals was the philatelic press. Counterfeit stamps were of great interest to collectors and they did not hesitate to share their stories of discovery in the philatelic press. Digging through these papers you can find little gems sprinkled here and there. One such gem indicates that this activity possibly existed long before 1895. It was reported by Philip H. Ward Jr. in *Mekeel's Weekly Stamps News* of December 26, 1952:

> We have just run across a letter written during 1863 in which a postmaster in Michigan writes to the Inspection Office of the Post Office Department in regards to counterfeit stamps being found on the letters passing through his office. This certainly comes as news to us and doubt very much whether a single copy of these counterfeits now exists. It was evidently a counterfeit of the regular 3c stamp of 1861, which was then current for paying letter postage. The letter reads as follows:

Post Office at
Mason, Ingham Co. Michigan
Oct. 22nd 1863

Chief Clerk, Inspection Office,

Enclosed I send you a sample of the counterfeit postage stamps that are in circulation, some here. They are received principally from the army. The Post Masters in those Southern Offices apparently not having noticed them yet. The one enclosed was obtained of a furloughed soldier from the 12th Michigan Infantry, now stationed in the South West. The letter was sent by him for mailing at this office, by a person named Hugh Neal, of Co. G. 12 Mich. Inf. The bearer had several letters for mailing to other offices with similar stamps upon them. He stated that they were sold to the soldiers by the Sutlers following the Army, and that no one there so far as he knows had yet detected them. The Sutlers name can be obtained undoubtedly by addressing said Neal. A great many letters have been received at this office from that direction paid with these stamps, marked upon the Post-bills "Paid by Stamps." I do not know what course to take with such letters.

Yours Very Respectfully
D. B. Harrington
Postmaster

As common as the counterfeiting of coins and currency was between 1865 and 1895, does it not seem reasonable that like-minded individuals would have also turned their attention to the common postage stamp?

2

Let's Do an Encore – Chicago 1896

You know, sometimes criminals are really, really dumb. What happened next shows that, yes, people with a criminal inclination did apparently read the newspapers, and they got ideas from them. Common sense should have also told them that just maybe Chicago was not the place to try a postal counterfeiting endeavor.

No sooner had the 1895 case been wrapped up when postal revenue again found itself under attack. The existence of this case would contribute to the lore and misinformation that would eventually envelop the story of the 1895 case. This second case would receive nowhere near the publicity the first one did. Over time the few facts that did become known to the public were distorted and spilled over to confuse what had happened in 1895. Once in print these distortions became "legitimized," and in the public's mind, became the accepted truth.

One example of this appeared in 1963 in an article written by Philip Ward for *Mekeel's Weekly Stamp News*:

> About the same time [as the 1895 Chicago Counterfeit], similar counterfeits were located in Buffalo, New York and these are known as the "Buffalo Prints." The stamps are somewhat similar to the Chicago prints; the design is smaller and the head of Washington somewhat cramped in an oval 14 mm wide, the former fake measuring 14 ¼ mm. The impression is overinked, giving a blurred appearance. Both varieties are in the carmine of the genuine stamps. We have never seen nor heard of a multiple of this Buffalo variety, nor have we seen a used copy. In fact, not over a half dozen copies have come to our attention. As a result of these counterfeits, the Bureau of Engraving and Printing immediately made arrangements to print our stamps on watermarked paper, hoping to make more difficult the work of the counterfeiter. We do not believe more stamps were made to defraud the government until about 1922.

Ward was misinformed on just about every count except the

description of the second stamp, and thus misinformed his readers. The location of the second case was the same as the first: Chicago, Illinois. Here is the story of what actually happened.

For Captain James E. Stuart, 1895 was a busy year. He had played a leading and very public role in the investigation of the first identified U.S. postal counterfeiting case. As the agent in charge of the Chicago office of the Bureau of Postal Inspectors, his daily responsibilities were no small matter.

The postal inspectors were responsible for overseeing the operations of all the post offices in the Chicago region. In the area of criminal investigation, Stuart's inspectors were charged with investigating mail theft, postal robberies, train robberies, burglaries of post offices, and use of the mail to defraud the public. In 1895, Stuart's office received 14,116 new cases for investigation. This was on top of the 3,607 cases that were still open and carried over from 1894. His inspectors had closed 14,424 cases, arrested 376 offenders, and recovered more than $45,000 for the government. Among these arrests they counted not only the Chicago counterfeiters, but also two groups of armed robbers, and at least one gang of postal burglars.

Both Captain Stuart and Captain Porter of the Secret Service had received a great deal of recognition for their work in arresting the Chicago postal counterfeiters. That case had yet to be concluded in court when one day Porter walked into Stuart's office and announced his suspicions that another counterfeit stamp was being sold on the street. This visit was triggered by information he had received from William W. DeWees – the same man who, one year earlier, had ordered and received a shipment of discounted U.S. 2-cent Washington stamps from Canada. The day after that delivery, Porter had walked into DeWees' office and seized the items as evidence. When in early April 1896 DeWees was again offered discounted postage – once burned is forewarned. DeWees did not wait for Porter. He literally ran to see the agent.

Stuart was busily involved in the routine investigative and administrative responsibilities of his office; it was decided this new investigation would be directed by Porter. Besides, Stuart may have felt there was such a thing as too much notoriety. In just the preceding four months he had been involved in two shooting incidents[9]. Still his inspectors would be involved. To help Porter in this investigation, Stuart assigned a number of inspectors to work with the Secret Service. Others were assigned to monitor incoming mail. If bogus stamps were again being used in the mail, the best place to identify them would be on the Chicago Post Office sorting tables.

Porter, like a spider in the center of his web, manipulated the different strands of the investigation. To assist with fieldwork, he called in another Secret Service agent from Indianapolis, and also drew from the local U.S. Marshal's office. As a face that might be unknown to local criminals, Deputy U.S. Marshal Logan was assigned to take up occupancy in DeWees' office. His assignment was to wait for the return of the two young men who were offering to sell stamps to DeWees.

One of the major problems in the first counterfeit investigation had been the premature publicity the case received in the tabloids. Porter was determined he would avoid this complication in this new case. Only those individuals who had an absolute need to know were informed that an investigation was even going on. A seal of absolute silence was clamped over all of the investigators' activities.

The agents soon tentatively identified one of the young men who had offered to sell discounted stamps to DeWees. They traced him to a residence at 1802 North Western Avenue, but their timing was unfortunate. Their suspect had already moved on. The search continued for his new location, and it only intensified when it was discovered that in his personal effects had been printing equipment.

Hard work and persistence eventually brought their reward. On April 14, the case broke open. Postal inspectors who were checking the Chicago mail found 600 letters bearing a new counterfeit 2-cent postage stamp. That same afternoon, one of the suspects who had previously offered to sell DeWees discounted postage, returned to conclude the sale. Deputy Marshal Logan listened while the negotiations took place, and when the counterfeit stamps were finally produced and money changed hands, Logan announced who he was

---

9   In one incident Stuart was en route to a masquerade ball when he witnessed a robbery and homicide. In his party costume and waving his cane, Stuart exited a streetcar into a hail of gunfire to apprehend the suspects. The local press loved it. I suspect that Washington was not so amused. Stuart was probably on a very short leash.

and placed the young man under arrest.

They soon established that this was not a criminal mastermind with whom they were dealing. The individual in custody was identified as William B. Peters, and when searched, Logan found his pockets were full of bogus stamps. Captain Porter was immediately notified of this arrest: yet even in his rush to get to the scene and question the young man he did not forget the seal of silence he had placed on this investigation. Before he rushed out of his office he posted a large sign on the door. It read: "It is no use for you to ask anybody about this building where I am, for they do not know."

Secret or not, the press soon began to hear rumors that there was another counterfeit stamp investigation under way. Newspaper reporters descended on both Porter's office and that of the Chicago Post Office. On their arrival, they were greeted with a wall of silence at both locations. At the post office, a classic form of bureaucratic runaround was employed. All reporters were politely referred to Postmaster Hesing. The only problem was that Hesing was conveniently out of town, and would not be back for some time. At Porter's office, the cold response was to invite all counterfeiters to step right in, and an agent could process their surrender. Otherwise, all questions on any topic would have to wait for Porter's return.

When he joined Logan, Porter began to grill Peters. He soon determined that these were not world-class criminals he was dealing with, and a full confession was soon extracted. Peters identified and implicated all the members of the gang. He then took the agents to his new lodging where they seized an additional 5,000 stamps. Peters was then given new lodging in the city jail. A stand-up guy he definitely was not.

In Peters' confession, he identified John Voney and Alpha J. Bodkin as his accomplices. Voney was found on Jackson Street at Skaley's Bucket Shop. Taken into custody, another package of stamps was found on his person. In searching for Bodkin, Porter went to the Pauline Hoyt Formula Company at 504 Van Buren Street. The 600 letters bearing the counterfeit stamps found in the Chicago mail all bore this return address.

At 504 Van Buren, the questioned address, Porter did not find a thriving business. When he walked in the door, he found a desk, three chairs, and a brass drum of chemicals with Bodkin's name printed on it. Bodkin was not there, but Porter was able to find Pauline Hoyt. She worked in another office in this building, and told the officer she really had no connection with Mr. Bodkin. She did know him and had given him permission to use her name in conducting his business. Later that night Porter did find Bodkin, and he then joined Voney and Peters in jail. Each prisoner was subjected to intensive questioning and before long the agent had extracted the complete story.

It was established that Peters was the engraver who did most of the plate work. Voney was both a lithographer and an engraver and his job was to assist Peters when it was time to make the printing plates. The stamps were then printed and perforated by all three of the conspirators. Using a lithographic stone, they had run off 20,000 stamps before they had erased the impression.

When the government announced the arrest of these three subjects, a Mr. M. E. Tracy came forward and contacted Captain Porter. Tracy worked as an express man and told the officer he knew the subjects who were being held. Besides that, he believed he had something Captain Porter might have an interest in. It turned out that after the stamps had been printed, Peters had hired him to move and then store some items. What Tracy led the officer to was a printing press, paper, pink printing ink, and five lithographing stones.

On April 16, the prisoners were taken before the U.S. commissioners where all three waived their right to a preliminary hearing. The three young men knew they needed no preview of the government's case. The night they had been arrested, Porter let them know just how solid the government's case was and how much trouble they were in. The trio knew their only hope was to throw themselves on the mercy of the court.

The defendants' cooperation had some effect. A bond of $1,000 was set for each defendant. On May 13, Captain Porter then went before a federal grand jury to present the government's case. To no one's surprise, the grand jury promptly returned a "true bill." William B. Peters, John Voney, and Alpha J. Bodkin were indicted on the following counts:

1. Counterfeiting 5,000 postage stamps.

2. On April 13, 1896, possession of 5,000 counterfeit postage stamps with the intent to use the same in the U.S. mail.

3. On April 14, 1896, placing 500 counterfeit stamps on letters and depositing said letters in the post office of the United States for mailing.

On May 22, Bodkin and Voney pleaded guilty to the charges. Bodkin was sentenced to serve three months of hard labor at the Illinois State Reformatory. Voney was sentenced to five months of hard labor in the Kane County Jail. As the mastermind behind this criminal enterprise, Peters feared what his fate might be. He requested a delay in his court proceedings. This was granted, and a new trial date was scheduled for November 14. When that fateful day arrived, all the interested parties were in the courtroom with one exception – Peters had fled the state.

A federal fugitive warrant was filed for Peters and the following year he was picked up in New York state on other charges. The Illinois authorities and Agent Porter briefly considered bringing him back to stand trial. In the end, it was decided to let him stay in a New York jail. Illinois was quite happy to export its criminals to other states. On May 14, 1897, an order was entered striking the case from the Illinois criminal docket with leave to reinstate. In the legal vernacular, this meant that if Peters was released in New York and had the poor judgment to return to Illinois, the old counterfeiting charges could be resurrected if he again appeared on law enforcement radar.

For an apparently amateur endeavor, the 1896 Chicago counterfeit was not all that badly executed. It foreshadowed what the government would face many years in the future when young adults and even teens realized it was not all that hard to duplicate the government's products. The 1896 case was potentially a very dangerous scheme. In the judgment of the philatelic press, the stamp reproduction in this second attempt was quite good. It was considered to be a much better reproduction than the Chicago counterfeit of 1895. The downfall to this budding criminal enterprise was that the young entrepreneurs attempted to sell their product to an individual who had been burned buying counterfeit stamps only the year before. You could say that if there was one place in the U.S. where in 1896 a crook should have expected the public to watch out for counterfeit stamps, it would have been Chicago.

The timely investigations by the government's agents did much more than protect postal revenue from the effects of just a few bogus stamps. This was a conspiracy that was only beginning. The confessed intention of the counterfeiters was to make an even more exact copy of the legitimate item. They planned to resume production of the counterfeits in sheets of 100 stamps each. What the government had found was just the test printing.

Probable Stamp Being Counterfeited:
U.S. Scott 267

Printed in Chicago, Illinois during March 1896, this 2-cent counterfeit is quite rare due to its limited printing and distribution. One of the originals was found in the variety collection of a noted philatelist who shall remain anonymous at his request. Three other original examples of the stamp were found, all in criminal docket number 2679, United States vs. William B. Peters et al, in the Federal Archives and Record Center in Chicago. In this criminal complaint, each time the bogus stamp must be described, an actual specimen is glued on the page.

The counterfeits were printed from impressions on stone lithography plates. The number of stamps printed on each sheet is not known. The counterfeits are perf 12. The color of the counterfeit is pink rather than the carmine of the legitimate Type III printing. As this is a lithograph printing, the finely etched detail normally found in the oval and in the figure of Washington is absent. This counterfeit was printed on a watermarked paper. None of my sources can identify the nature of the watermark.

Watermarked Paper And Counterfeit Stamps

More needs to be said about the use of watermarked paper in stamp production. From 1895 until 1917, the Bureau of Engraving and Printing utilized watermarked paper in postage stamp production.

Over time, many stamp collectors and philatelic writers have made the assumption the government took this action as a direct result of the discovery of the first Chicago counterfeit stamp. That conclusion is incorrect. Governments have used watermarks to protect both their currency and postal products, but the decision to do so in the United States began long before the discovery of the first Chicago counterfeit.

The first Chicago counterfeit was discovered in early April 1895. Fewer than 30 days later, the new issue of government postage stamps came out printed on a watermarked paper. The date of issue for the watermarked 1-cent stamp was April 29 1895. The 2-cent was issued on May 2.

The use of watermarks in paper for security purposes is a device that cannot be accomplished overnight. First the design of the watermark had to be decided on – in itself no small feat in a government bureaucracy. With the issue of 1895, the double-lined "USPS" (United States Postage Stamp) watermark was adopted. Special rollers to impress the watermark into the paper pulp during the manufacturing process had to be contracted for and produced. Plus, the actual printing of the stamp design could begin only after the watermarked paper had been seasoned.

With rolls of properly prepared and seasoned watermarked paper on hand, the printing of the stamps could begin. J.M. Bartels, in his *Washington Notes* of September 24, 1896, summarized the stamp production process of the time: "It takes about two weeks to finish a sheet of stamps from the time it is printed until it is ready for the vault. The ink is left at least a week to harden and the gum several days. No less than three times it is subjected to pressure. Three months is the average time for it to remain in the vault before it is issued."

From the aforementioned, it is obvious the discovery of counterfeit stamps in Chicago was not the impetus for U.S. stamps to be printed on watermarked paper. On a purely practical basis the time required for the various elements that go into the production makes that scenario impossible. It was by coincidence – albeit a helpful one – not a swift reaction by the POD, that new watermarked stamps followed so quickly in the wake of the counterfeits.

When the counterfeit stamps were discovered, the postal

officials in Washington, D.C., must have been dismayed. The existence of this criminal activity would have only reinforced their view that using watermarks was the correct and necessary thing to do. Once in place, watermarks on U.S. postage stamps would continue for the next 20 years.

In 1996, watermarked paper would make a big comeback, and it was with United States currency. For some time our currency had been under serious attack, and one of the security features found in the 1996 $100 bill was the watermark of Franklin's profile. As each denomination had been redesigned, a watermark would be included.[10]

A Mystery Still Remains

One day a friend was doing research at the National Archives in Washington D.C. While leafing through documents, he made an unexpected discovery. Buried in correspondence was an envelope entitled "Solicitation to sell counterfeit stamps." Knowing of my interest in counterfeit stamps, he shared his discovery with me.

Inside the envelope he found a letter dated June 9, 1901, from the postal inspector assigned to Portland, Oregon. It was his report to the inspector in charge for Spokane and it reported suspected criminal activity in his jurisdiction:

Sir:

I have the honor to hand you herewith three letters addressed to the postmasters at Astoria, Grass Valley, and Eugene, Oregon, respectively, all written by the same person, but signed by different names, and all requesting answers to be addressed to the same place

Vic: "69 North 3rd St. Portland, Oregon."

In these communications an offer is made to sell these postmasters large quantities of counterfeit postage stamps at 20-cents on the dollar. The place given as the address of the writer of these letters is a "Men's Resort," a sort of a charity reading room in the slums of Portland, known as the "North End," where all the dissolute characters "hang out" during the daytime.

I have a similar letter addressed to the P.M. at Oregon City, Oregon,

---

10 An excellent discussion on the problem that a watermark poses to the counterfeiter is presented in *The Art of Making Money* by Jason Kersten.

which I will retain as I had him answer it and am now watching for the person to take the reply. He signed the Oregon City letter
            "Samuel N. Johnes."

    As soon as this matter was arranged I went to the Chief of Police, with whom I am on familiar terms, and he at once detailed two of his Detectives to assist me in keeping the watch for the party in question. As one of these detectives works in the "North End" all the time he is a familiar sight there so it was easy for him, without danger of arousing suspicion, as would a stranger, to arrange matters so we could tell when the letter was taken. In this "Resort" all letters for strangers are placed in a rack on the wall, and Detective Weiner had my test so placed that we could see it by simply passing the open door and were therefore not obliged to enter the place at all.

    We kept a vigilant watch on the place all the time it was open yesterday and will do so today and tomorrow before removing the test, and of course hope it will be taken away that we may capture the individual who desires to make postmasters rich so easily.

    There is a suspicion in the minds of the City Detectives working with me on the case that the person wanted is a ex-convict recently liberated from the Penitentiary at Salem, Oregon, and who is now rooming within a block of the "Resort" in a cheap lodging house. He appeared on the scene twice yesterday and by his actions, and hesitancy when passing the door, it seemed quite evident to us he wanted to enter but was suspicious.

            This for Jacket.
            Very Respectfully,
            E.C. Clement
            Inspector

    Exactly what is going on here is anyone's guess. No further information could be found in either postal records or the National Archives. This could have been just a con man's attempt to entice money out of less-than-honest postmasters. Similar schemes are called "Green Goods" operations and were very common at the turn of the last century. Then again, we could be dealing with an actual attempt to distribute counterfeit stamps. The golden grail for the counterfeiter of stamps would be to slip your product into the normal distribution chain of a post office.

If this was not a fraud, this could be an entirely unknown new counterfeit. Then again, it is known that in the first Chicago counterfeit case an unknown number of stamps were sent to western destinations. Not only was this substantiated in the news reports of the case, but best of all, two actual envelopes bearing the first Chicago counterfeit stamp and West Coast postmarks have been identified. Just because there is no public record of a West Coast printing, that does not mean it did not occur.

In my mind, there is one point that gives this report legitimacy. That is the price at which the stamps were being offered. From an investigator's point of view, you can usually judge how close you are to a printing operation based on the percentage off of face value it is commanding. When you are at 20 to 30 percent off of face, you usually are very close to the press. This holds true for both currency and stamps.

You might want to take a closer look at those vintage stamps in your collection. You just might have a counterfeit variety that has not yet been identified.

Counterfeiters Brought to Justice?

Through the years, if the general public has been unaware of the existence of postal counterfeits, one segment of the population that did take note were the stamp collectors. They may have first had their doubts, but when they climbed on board it was full speed ahead. Most likely this explains why it has frequently been a stamp collector who brings these items to the attention of the government. That, and the fact that the only ones who really examined stamps with a critical eye was the collector.

In response to the collectors' appetite for news on counterfeiting activity, it wasn't surprising that stories about this crime began to appear in the philatelic press. One such story appeared in the December 1, 1897, issue of the *Herald Exchange*, a philatelic monthly published in New York from 1896 to 1900. The following is a condensed version from the original.

Counterfeiters Brought to Justice
An Important Arrest:
Being a Full Account of the Recent
Manufacture and Sale of Bogus
Postage Stamps.

A Reporter of the "Herald Exchange"
Liberally Paid for the Service He
Rendered in Bringing About the
Capture and Conviction of the
Noted Henry Krammer and His Men

The latest and undoubtedly one of the greatest schemes for manufacturing bogus stamps is probably fresh in the minds of a certain few collectors, dealers and others in Greater New York, even though the attitude of the Department has been that no information be given to the public concerning the recent capture and confiscation of all plates and printing equipment.

However, as much credit is due the Herald Exchange, and its agents, for so successfully bringing the gang of counterfeiters to justice, and as no instructions have, as yet, been received stating that it will be a breach to publish the particulars, it is intended to herewith present to the readers of the Herald Exchange, the first full account of the affair, the details of which have been carefully summed up by P. Robertson Lee, reporter temporarily representing the Herald Exchange in the acquirements of philatelic news happenings in the metropolitan district. His report is:

On November 10th, a young man, apparently about thirty years of age, called at my office, and handed me an introductory letter from a mutual friend. After a few rather formal and common place remarks, he explained the real cause of his visit, representing himself to be employed by a corporation handling a very large mail order business, and stated that a great many of their patrons made remittances in unused stamps. He said that while the company put to use a number of these stamps in their own mailing department, the receipts far exceeded their requirement of low value stamps for postal purposes. He further explained. ... That if it could dispose of all the stamps the firm could not use. ... He would sell me them at 20% discount from face value. ... He replied that heretofore they had had to dispose of more than one thousand dollars worth every month, but that in view of the approaching holiday season, a much larger amount than this would be received and have to be sold. ...

I was ready to jump at this man's proposition, for I thought I saw a comparatively easy way of making in the neighborhood of two hundred dollars on every thousand dollars worth sold. I had not the least suspicion that my newly made acquaintance, Mr. J.B. Bown, was anything but sincere in his statements, so when he proposed to let me have $500 worth the following day, for which I was to pay him $400, I readily agreed.

The next day, true to his promise, Mr. Bown met me and after counting out the stamps to my satisfaction, I gave him my check in payment. Then recollecting that I had in the banking firm of Davier, Greeke & Co. a warm friend, I called upon him and brought up the subject of stamps, with the result that before I left I had disposed of $300 worth at one percent discount. I began to think I was doing pretty fine in my new side occupation. And was all the more enthusiastic before night, for I had, in the afternoon succeeded in prevailing upon one of the large New York Daily papers to take the remaining $200 worth off of my hands on a basis of 5% discount from face value.

Early in the morning on the 12th, my telephone bell sounded sharply, and I may say that any hopes I had previously harbored with regard to becoming a millionaire by the sale of postage stamps, were rudely shattered by the receipt of such news as I heard over the wire, from my chum in the banking house that morning. He said the stamps were pronounced forgeries by a prominent New York expert; and he demanded an immediate interview with me.... I hurried around to Davier, Greeke & Co., and was soon in consultation with one of the partners, and also with an official representing the authorities. After settling with the firm for the stamps sold them, also forwarding a note to the New York paper, so that I might stop the use of the stamps from that source and have no trouble with them, my time was taken up with the officer of the Secret Association.

I gave him as full an account of the affair as I possibly could, describing Bown in detail, and then we proceeded to hunt him up, ostensibly for the purpose of purchasing some more of the stamps, but really to secure better evidence of his guilt. We experienced little difficulty in locating him. ... He seemed very much pleased, and did not hesitate to let us have several hundred dollars worth of the stamps. He appeared to have an inexhaustible supply, and so it turned out later. We paid him cash with marked bills, and secured the sheets of stamps. He was then asked out to dine with us. Hardly had we reached the street when the Inspector of the Secret Association, Mr. Skifford, threw open his outer coat, displayed his special badge, and placed Bown under arrest charging him with selling bogus stamps. He was, of course, highly indignant, saying his arrest was preposterous, and threatening us with the most direful results in case we proceeded further in our accusations. His talk made little, if any, impression on Skifford, who calmly walked his prisoner through a side street to the jail. ...

Skifford failed utterly in his attempt to have his prisoner make a confession. Bown had nothing to say, except that he was entirely innocent of the charge. ... Bown was not the man Skifford thought him to be; and both of us little imagined that we had in him, the great notorious crook, Henry Krammer, famed the world over for his exceeding daring in schemes to defraud. ...

I decided to put my reportorial powers to work and try and help the officials to find the headquarters of the men [with] whom Bown was thought to be associated. ... Skifford had taken a fancy to me, and offered to use his endeavors to have me liberally paid in case I could get evidence sufficient to warrant arresting any other parties.... in the scheme.

... I found a clue, which I justly thought would lead to still greater disclosures. I had the day before interviewed the party from whom Bown had procured his letter of introduction to me. And it was from this individual that I learned that Bown had a room in the Hotel Pryscile. ... I proceeded at once to the hotel, and inquired of the clerk in attendance for Bown. He said the latter was on a trip out of town. ... I engaged a room, being particular to see that it was right next to that of Bown's.... there was a door connecting the two rooms, and it was not long before I had the door unlocked and going through to Bown's room. ... Three dress suit cases immediately caught my eye, and ... having received a special commission from the authorities, I carefully worked with my bunch of keys, and easily opened first one, then all three of the cases, only to find them filled with wearing apparel. I was quite disappointed in finding nothing in the cases. ... After inspecting the room, I had about given up the thought of finding any evidence, when my eyes ran over to the cases again, and this time I noticed they seemed exceedingly wide, and I at once wondered how it took such large ones to accommodate such a small amount of clothing as I found them to contain. This gave me an idea; suppose the cases had false bottoms.

... I again opened them. ... Underneath was that which I had hoped to see – a space well filled with a variety of engraver's tools, plates, paper, etc. I took out the contents of the secret compartments and looked them over, after which I replaced them with the exception of a package of letters and telegrams. ... I withdraw to my own room. And spent half an hour or so in going over the correspondence, with the result that I collected enough data to warrant my bringing the whole matter before the Inspector of the Secret Association...

From the letters I ... learned that representatives were in Boston, Providence, Brooklyn, Philadelphia and Baltimore, and from a statement of the number of stamps sent out from headquarters, I concluded that in all there must be over one hundred thousand dollars worth of the stamps in the hands of agents.... I lost no time in finding Skifford, the Inspector, who in turn, after having secured the cases at the hotel, placed all the particulars before his superiors.... We had the satisfaction of knowing before night.... that the Providence and Baltimore agents had been found and arrested.

Meanwhile several detectives had been sent over to Astoria, Long Island, for the purpose of finding the "home office," as it were of the gang. ... I was detailed to go with the detectives, and do what I could to help them in their hunt. It was I who had found out about the Astoria plant, from certain papers secured in Bown's cases.... We went to Astoria; and walked for several minutes along Mine Road, until we reached number 618, the place indicated on the papers to be the headquarters.... Our party divided, one-half surrounding the building, the other half going in the front door. There were four detectives and myself on the outside.... The detectives were, of course, well armed and prepared for almost any sort of reception. The officers who had gone inside the house came out in about five minutes, and reported that no one was there, although evidence was plentiful that until very recently men had been at work printing and gumming stamps, for the form was still on the stone, and gummed sheets were in the oven.... It was Inspector Skifford who finally decided that it would do no harm to wait a while, and see what would turn up, so we all went inside the building, men stationed at the doors leading to the street and rear entrance. We did not have to wait long for developments. The men had only gone out for breakfast!

At 8:30 a.m., footsteps were heard on the porch and then a key was turned in the front door, and two men walked in – on the arms of three of our big detectives. There was no possible chance for the men to escape them, and when they saw such odds, they offered no resistance. Handcuffs were snapped on them, after which they were led into the rear room where we had previously found a complete apparatus for making counterfeit stamps. We had difficulty getting anything out of the men, but upon bringing our persuasive powers to bear, it was not long before one of them offered to make a clean breast of the affair, inasmuch as he knew about it. After one of the men had shown willingness toward confession, the other was even more anxious than he to disclose the facts which he knew.... They claimed to be employed as ordinary lithographers on a regular salary, and said that while they knew the business was not an honest one, that because of the peculiar way in which they became interested in it, they were afraid to do otherwise than they were instructed by the parties by whom they were hired.

At first Skifford was skeptical, and would not believe this story. ... Bown's name was mentioned to the men. ... They replied it was he who had induced them to take up the work. In fact, he superintended the whole business and looked after the agents, who had been old chums of his, and who had before been connected to such schemes. ... On the 21st of November, Bown and his pals ... were placed on trial, with the result that the leader received a sentence of twenty-five years in the penitentiary, and each of his men who had acted as agents on other cities were given 5 years, all with fines ranging from 500 dollars to 5000 dollars. ... My work was not overlooked, and the authorities presented me with a check for a very nice sum. I was also asked to accept a position as 2nd Ass't Inspector, but having a business occupying all my attention, outside of my regular reporting duties, I was forced to decline. ...

The authorities will no doubt be furious when this article is brought to their notice, but I guess after they look it over, and see that it is nothing more than a **mere dream**, affairs in their department of labor will once more drift along in the same manner as of old. The readers of the Herald Exchange are thanked for so kindly reading this STORY. If there are any other counterfeiting schemes on foot in this or any other country, you may rest assured that the Herald Exchange will give full account, because they have a man detailed for just that sort of work.

The telltale boldfaced words in the final paragraph are the truth of the matter: that this was a work of fiction, a well-executed figment of the writer's imagination, playing up to the public's urge to read more about the new and exciting subject of postal counterfeits. Ironically, in producing a fictional tale, the author came much closer to capturing the reality of the first two cases (and many more to follow) than did many writers in the philatelic and general press in reporting the actual events.

Afterthoughts

The original Chicago case was a well thought-out criminal conspiracy. The representation of the stamp was more than adequate. If the effort had been confined to Thomson's business, this scheme could have gone on for years without discovery – if ever.

Printing the stamps in Chicago and running the distribution from another location showed originality. Advertising the stamps as discounted postage in newspapers offered an opportunity for widespread distribution. The downfall was that they also advertised in Chicago, which had a knowledgeable and large stamp collecting community. It did not help the criminals that they ran up against two of the most effective criminal investigators of that day, Captain Stuart of the post office and Captain Porter of the Secret Service.

The search of Mrs. Lacy's apartment presents some thoughts.

Rule No. 1: You probably do not want your press and perforator in a second floor residential apartment. Even if it is a small letter type press and small perforator, it is going to generate noise and vibration. If you do not control your surroundings it is going to aggravate your neighbors.

Rule No. 2: If you are going to print stamps (or currency) in your residence, make sure you totally destroy the waste product. It is amazing the number of times the authorities are called when the garbage man finds printing waste in the trash.

With the second Chicago case, for an amateur endeavor it showed promise. The mistake they made was to launch their enterprise in Chicago. Not only were the authorities aware of the concept of counterfeit stamps, but with the notoriety of the first case so fresh in everybody's mind, virtually every person in Chicago was as well. Then, they really had not thought out a distribution plan. They tried to sell their product on the street, and one person they approached had been burned the first time around. From beginning to end they were making it up as they went along.

A Forgotten History

The Secret Service we know today has little if any resemblance to what it was when it was created. Growing out of the Civil War (known to some as the war of Northern Aggression) it was a creation of the bureaucracy. It was not authorized by congress or executive order. A Treasury Secretary just did it.

In the 1860s there was no national paper currency. The government coined currency; they did not print it. Two hundred state and local banks issued their own paper money, and it is estimated that at least 80 percent of it was counterfeit[11]. When the Treasury Secretary decided to address this problem, he concluded the best way to catch a thief was with a thief. At least 50 percent of the agents put into the field were criminals themselves. This was not a system destined to gain the confidence of either the public or the judiciary.

The first 40 or so years of this agency was spotty at best. In the 1890s men of both integrity and administrative ability began to appear in the ranks personified by Captain Porter and Chief Hazen. Senior agents at the direction of Chief Hazen were instructed to develop press relations and "polish" the public image of the service. It had its effect and by the 1920s the service was held in high regard. The service would still have its share of cowboys, but they were honest cowboys, and they produced results.

The roots of the Inspection Service go back to the early days of the national post office. Although political patronage played a part in almost all postal appointments, unlike postmasters, when

---

11 The Confederacy issued paper currency and had the same plague of counterfeiting that the nation as a whole did. On more than one occasion the counterfeiter was caught because his printing was better than that put out by Richmond.

administrations changed from one party to another, inspectors were not removed. The end result was that in short order the only ones in the post office who knew the answers were the inspectors.

Today, political patronage is in disrepute. For most of the history of our country that was how the national government functioned. Some appointments were deadwood others were the best of the best. Captain Stuart fell into that latter category. He arrived in this country as an immigrant child. With Lincoln's call to arms he enlisted as a private in the 21st Wisconsin. He ended the war with the rank of captain as a veteran of many actions. With the Spanish-American War he went back into uniform, and as a major, commanded the 2nd Illinois Infantry in Cuba. Before returning to his duties as a postal inspector, he set up the Puerto Rico mail service. He died in 1931 with the military rank of Brigadier General. He had outlived his friend Thomas Porter by five years. Stuart was typical of the men who populated the ranks of the inspectors.

Neither the Secret Service nor the Inspection Service were overwhelmed with manpower. As a result, out of necessity agents of each service frequently worked together.

3

Thinking Outside the Box

The Counterfeit Postal Cards of 1902

For some time the Post Office Department had suspected that its postal cards were being counterfeited. In the spring of 1902, these suspicions would be confirmed by events on the ground. Counterfeit postal cards would be found.

On April 23, 1902, newspapers in both New York and Boston reported "Spurious Postals Flood Country." On the preceding day, the New York General Post Office had issued a warning notice to every postal facility in that city alerting their employees to be on the lookout for counterfeit postal cards. This warning notice was immediately picked up by newspaper reporters. The notice they published read:

> This office is advised by the Post Office inspector in charge of this division that he has been informed of the circulation of a counterfeit postal card, which is described as follows:
>
> The card appears to be a counterfeit. The top of the name line runs together, while in the genuine card it is spaced. The lines in Jefferson's face are coarse and broken and the wreath is not uniform. The word "Jefferson" is in light face type, while in the genuine bold face type is used.
>
> The paper on which the card is printed is a coated paper never used for postal cards. The whole appears to be a copy from an old worn plate.

The *New York Herald* commented, "Counterfeiting of postal cards is a new industry. Post Office officials say that the probable reason for the counterfeit postals [postal cards] is that business houses are using increased numbers of them every year." The article went on to say counterfeit postal cards were being discovered in mail postmarked from nearly every part of the United States.

No sooner did the newspaper account of the warning notice hit the street than the focus of the government's investigation shifted to Chicago. As before, it was inspector James E. Stuart who would discover the needle in the haystack.

Early in April 1902, Stuart had begun to visit printing houses that specialized in the enameling of waste postal cards. At that time, there was no provision in postal regulations for the post office to buy back damaged or misprinted card stock that had not been used in the mail. If a business had waste card stock, the only way it could recover some of their investment was to sell these items to a recycler. The recycler in turn would cover any old printing with an enamel coating, usually a bronze, silver, or clay covering. These cards could then have a new message superimposed over the old, and the items would be ready for reuse. This was a legitimate business, and throughout the country there were many firms that specialized in this activity.

When he visited the enamelers, Stuart was either acting on a suspicion he had, or he was following a directive from his superiors in Washington. What triggered these visits, newspaper accounts would later report, was a suspect postal card that had been found in the Chicago mail. This card had the new Jefferson portrait, and the overall printing had been carefully done. The suspicious element was the badly blurred lettering of "Jefferson" in the vignette.

It appears that Stuart began to focus on one E. Louis Smith as a prime suspect. He had identified Smith as a major supplier and dealer in postal card stock. Under Stuart's direction, his agents began to dig into the background of this individual, and it would become apparent that he was indeed the counterfeiter.

The agents found that Smith was not your common, everyday criminal. This was a respected young man in the community who had no hint or suspicion of criminal activity associated with his name. He roomed with a good family at 3012 Wabash Street and was engaged to be married to a respectable young lady. Before going into his own business, Smith had been with the Chicago Board of Trade and was considered a successful young man. A common refrain heard was, if anything, he was generous to a fault.

When a discreet surveillance was set up, it was soon established that Smith rented an office in the Rialto Building in downtown Chicago. At that location he conducted a business under the name of the Nerve Seed Remedy Company. Common for that day, the commodity he was pedaling was a "nerve restorer." What the surveillance also discovered was that Smith also seemed to be spending an inordinate amount of time in room 10 of the Hayman Office Building on South Water Street. His activities there were unknown.

The record is far from clear exactly how Stuart put all the pieces together, but in very short order he knew this was the person for whom he was looking. On April 24, he went to the Rialto Building to first interview, and then to arrest this young man. Under questioning, Smith acknowledged that he had been buying waste postal cards from local businesses, and used these items for his own advertisements. Being an astute businessman, he soon recognized the business potential of these items and, yes, he then developed a sideline of supplying his excess coated cards to other customers.

The first rule in conducting any successful interrogating is that you have to put the suspect "at ease." You have to get him talking. Let him tell his story. Then, and only then, do you begin to hit the suspect with the facts – or what you believe are the facts. At some point in Stuart's interview it turned into an interrogation, and Stuart informed Smith that while they were talking he had agents searching the Water Street address. Smith surely recognized that his goose was cooked, and he began to tell Stuart the truth.

Even the most hardened criminal will frequently break down in an interrogation, and this individual was not a hardened criminal. One weapon Stuart may have employed was his knowledge that this was basically a decent young man. Stuart played on his heartstrings. Knowing that Smith was romantically involved, and planned to be married in just a few weeks, one can imagine Stuart asking how he was going to feel when his fiancée's name was dragged through the mud by the local press.

Newspaper reports stated that when Smith was confronted with the impact his actions could have on the reputation of his fiancée, he cracked. Being an "Honorable Man," he completely broke down. The *Chicago Daily News* gave the following melodramatic account of what happened next:

> Louis Smith Visits Sweetheart After
> Confessing Guilt – Authorities

Find 800,000 Cards

Today, walking between two United States deputies, Louis Smith who wrote out a confession to Inspector James E. Stuart that for two years he had been counterfeiting postal cards in room 10, Hayman building, at 152 South Water street, was marched up the stairs of a north side residence and into the presence of the young woman to whom he was engaged to be married this summer. The confessed counterfeiter placed $300 in bills in the hands of his fiancée, who stood in wonder.

It Was Their Wedding Cash

"It is the money you gave me to keep for you until we were married," said Smith, huskily.

The girl took the money. "What does it mean?" she asked.

Smith choked. "It means that I am going to prison instead of to the altar. No. Don't come near me. I'm not fit for you to know." Then turning quickly to the officers he demanded: "Take me away. I should not have come."

When Smith was taken back to Stuart's office, he made an unusual request, thereby demonstrating he was basically a decent young man. He asked if he could return to the account holders a number of checks he had received for orders he would now be unable to fill. Stuart allowed him to do this. An illustration appeared in the newspaper of Smith at a desk, scratching his name off nearly a score of checks received from businesses all across the country. It amounted to several hundred dollars' worth of enameled postal cards for which he could no longer make delivery.

Smith's confession laid out the details of what is believed to be the largest fraud perpetrated on the revenues of the U.S. Post Office Department up to that time. He acknowledged that for two years he had been printing, selling, and distributing counterfeit postal cards; he figured that the quantities he had made and sold numbered in the millions. Smith insisted he had conducted this criminal enterprise entirely on his own, and that no other person knew of, or had assisted him in any of his illegal activities.

The investigation determined that Smith's only employee was

a woman stenographer working in his office at the Rialto Building. She handled the correspondence with companies ordering Smith's postal cards. Smith professed she had no idea anything was amiss with her employer or the business he was conducting. The stories told by both agreed, and she was soon released by the authorities without any charges placed against her.

Questioning the rental manager for the Hayman Building, agents found Smith had been renting room 10 for the last two years. This was the room where the printing press had been located, and where Smith had printed the spurious cards. Everything Stuart learned supported his prisoner's story that in two years of renting the room, Smith was the only person who had ever entered this location.

Under arrest, Smith then took Stuart to his lodgings where he turned over a dozen or more engraved plates and 50,000 bogus coated postal cards. The inspectors who searched the South Water Street offices found other engraved plates, a printing press, a cutting machine, and more than 60,000 completed counterfeit postal cards. Smith then led Stuart to Dearborn and Madison streets, the location of the Prent Printing Company. There, agents picked up an additional 30,000 counterfeit cards that were about to be enameled. (Different sources report different totals for the number of cards seized. I have used the figures cited by the *Chicago Tribune* on April 25, 1902. The *Chicago Daily News* would report the number as being between 800,000 and 1 million).

For what might be considered an amateur operation, many of the details of Smith's enterprise were truly innovative. Smith, for example, was not an engraver, and his solution to this little problem was to outsource. To make his printing plates, the easy solution would have been to turn to the criminal class, a course of action that had led to the downfall of many counterfeiting enterprises. Not uncommonly, many of these individuals were also in the employment of the government. They traded information for their freedom. Smith's solution was to employ many different legitimate engravers in piecework. Each individual was hired to make a different item, and none of these individuals suspected for a moment that he had become a party to any illegal enterprise.

One engraver was employed to make a multi-sectioned plate

purportedly for an invitation that had a number of Jefferson heads on it. Another made a plate with various individual pieces including the words "United States of America." Other engravers were hired to produce plates with other words and features found on the face of legitimate postal cards. Smith then picked and chose among all of the individual pieces, and like a jigsaw puzzle, he clamped them in the correct pattern in a holder called a printer's chase. When all the pieces were together, he had his printing plate.

Another part of Smith's genius was that he was not satisfied to simply produce and then sell bogus postal cards. He carried his scheme one step further. First, in many cases an advertisement would be printed on the reverse. The intent of this ad was to support the impression that the cards taken to be enameled were the result of printers' waste or print overruns. No one would suspect the cards themselves were bogus to begin with.

Besides helping to protect from being discovered, this extra step of printing a false advertisement also enabled Smith to increase his potential market and profit margin. By selling what appeared to be a legitimate postal product, he was not forced to deal with either unscrupulous business houses or individuals who would knowingly buy counterfeit items. Then also, when you are dealing in the counterfeits of any item, your product is normally sold at a steep discount. Smith was able to sell his fake products at the full price that legitimate items would command.

Until the government interrupted his activity, Smith was enjoying a very lucrative enterprise, or at least that is my contention. After purchasing a printing press and contracting for the engraving, his business expenses were negligible – all he needed was raw card stock and printing ink. To enamel cards, the Prent Printing Company was charging Smith $1.70 per 1,000 cards. Smith, in turn, sold his end product to his customers for one cent each, or 1,000 for $10. An additional selling point Smith pushed was that not only would he supply the cards to his customers, but also at no additional charge, he would print the advertisement of their choice on the enameled product. He had no difficulty finding customers.

Stuart documented that the Prent Company was but one of a number of enameling concerns that Smith had employed. At the

Prent Company, their records showed they alone had enameled more than 700,000 postal cards for Smith. Stuart would publicly speculate that Smith had produced and caused to be put into circulation at least 1 million counterfeit cards. Some sources would speculate the true number was actually closer to 10 million.

In a *Chicago Tribune* (April 25, 1902) article was a very interesting statement: "Smith told Inspector Stuart that he had learned the (art) [of making counterfeit postal cards] years ago from a man for whom he had worked."[12] If true, the implications of this statement were staggering. In the research of postal stationery expert Frank B. Stratton, he identified some of Smith's handiwork going back to as early as 1899. This raises an interesting question. Was he working independently, or was he still "learning his art" from his mentor? Regardless of the time frame, his story of learning his craft means that somewhere there was another counterfeiter who to our knowledge has never been exposed or identified.

When they got around to doing an inventory of Smith's effects they found thousands of legitimate U.S. postal cards. Some of these items had been in circulation since 1897. This discovery raises a number of questions. Was Smith a philatelist at heart, who admired the artistry of the government's legitimate printings? More

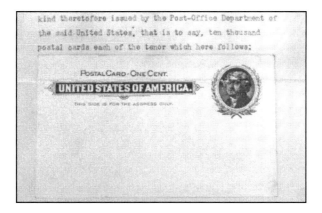

---

12 This has the ring of truth. In the world of counterfeiting, it is very common for an established "master" to take a younger prodigy under his wings and teach him the trade. Counterfeiting is a skill that is frequently handed down from one generation to another.

likely, he was examining these items with an eye to their potential for reproduction. Then again, maybe he already had.

Appearing before the United States commissioner, Smith waived the formality of a hearing. Stuart went before the Federal Grand Jury on April 25, and indicted E. Louis Smith on four counts of counterfeiting U.S. postal cards. To the eternal benefit of researchers, Stuart showed he was a creature of habit. As in the two previous stamp cases, each time the spurious cards had to be described in this indictment, an actual example was affixed to the document.

The federal government occasionally does learn from prior mistakes. In the two previous stamp cases, when placed on bond, defendants had fled the state. In his case, Smith's bail was set purposely high at $10,000, and when he failed to post this bond, he was locked up in the Cook County jail.

On May 23, 1902, E. Louis Smith was arraigned on charges of manufacturing plates for the counterfeiting of United States postal cards, and for the counterfeiting of United States postal cards for use in the mail. He entered a guilty plea, and on June 2, 1902, he was sentenced to two years of hard labor in the Illinois State Penitentiary.

Seldom noted for speedy or decisive action, the postal authorities in Washington suddenly came alive with activity. Almost concurrent with Smith's indictment, the Chicago postmaster received instructions from the Post Office Department that henceforth prohibited bronzed or other coated postal cards for use in the mail. Virtually overnight this prohibition was then established as national policy. The screams of anguish this generated can only be imagined.

Many businesses and legitimate dealers in coated postal cards suddenly found their entire inventory of such items not only worthless but also now illegal. Being hit in their pocketbooks, legitimate card dealers and businessmen who used this commodity ran to their local politicians. The political protest this generated soon caused the post office to again amend their position. A new directive went out extending the valid use of coated postal cards in the mail up to August 1, 1902. In July, the P.O.D. further changed existing regulations. This time it covered the redemption of spoiled postal cards. Finally, post offices were authorized to redeem spoiled postal card stock at a percentage of its face value.

After the immediate panic caused by the discovery of the counterfeit postal cards subsided, Major Reeve of the Post Office Stamp Division made a public announcement. Paraphrased in *Mekeel's*: Now that this problem had been addressed, the government's new position was that Smith's efforts were suddenly poor in imitation and execution. Reeve stated that "he could make a better one with a meat ax" and the department did not anticipate any serious trouble from this counterfeit. Today, we would call this statement official spin.

The only problem with this "official mindset" – and with Reeve's dismissive statement – is that this is an invitation to disaster. Counterfeiting is not a problem to be dismissed out of hand. In the case of the counterfeit postal cards, it would really be helpful to know how this discovery came about. Compared with the government's product, Smith's imitations frankly did not stand out as inferior products. At the time this case occurred, a private contractor, Albert Daggett, was producing the authorized postal cards issued and sold by the post office. In the philatelic world, the general consensus has been that Daggett's work was notorious for its poor workmanship. Smith's copies could and did easily pass for those being sold by the government.[13]

At the very least, a million of Smith's counterfeit postal cards were sold and used. One would think that in the hands of collectors you would find numerous examples of these items. That is not the case. Writing in *Postal Stationery* in 1971, Frank B. Stratton and Charles A. Fricke published the results of extensive research they had conducted. They managed to find 15 original counterfeit items. In their research they identified four different counterfeit plates that could be tied to Smith.

He is known to have duplicated postal cards UX-12, the 1-cent Jefferson issue of 1894; and UX-14, the 1-cent Jefferson of 1897. Smith's counterfeit UX-14 is most easily identified by the missing serifs on the second T in the word "STATES." The UX-12 cards are identifiable by the overall poor quality of printing found on them.

---

13 In the late 1970s, when postal inspectors began to seriously look for counterfeit postage meter impressions, they were instructed to watch for impressions of very good appearance: clean, clear, sharp meter impressions could be the hallmark of a counterfeit meter. If it is blurred and broken its legitimate. If it is clear and precise, it may be counterfeit.

The plate work looks worn, and the card stock is coarse and has a dark buff color. Possibly it was examples of this printing that first brought the counterfeits to the attention of authorities in New York and Boston.

Extensive research has been conducted into the products produced by E. Louis Smith by a number of noted philatelic experts. William Falberg published two articles in *Postal Stationery* that documents his identification of Smith's products. Other accounts have been published by Ken Lawrence and also Varro E. Tyler. In Tyler's *Linns* article he summarized the identifying characteristics of Smith's work.

Characteristics of the United States 1-cent Jefferson
Postal Card of 1897
Scott UX 14

Genuine:

    1. Distinct serifs on base of second "T" and at left base of "E" of "STATES"

    2. Most cards lack metallic or clay coating. Card stock is tan color.

Characteristics of all Smith forgeries:

    1. No visible serifs on base of second "T" and at left base of "E" of "STATES."

    2. Cards are coated on back, sometimes with additional printing, and less commonly on front. Card stock is dark tan to brownish.

Characteristics of four plates of Smith forgeries:

    Plate 1. Break in the thin oval frame line around the portrait at left, opposite the bridge of Jefferson's nose.

    Plate 2. Small white spots between the tops of "S" and "T" of "STATES" and near upper-left corner of "O" of "OF."

    Plate 3. Small black dot on this oval frame line around portrait at left, opposite Jefferson's eyebrow.

    Plate 4. (new) There is a slight doubling of the thin oval frame line around portrait at left, just opposite Jefferson's mouth. The thin line above the inscription is very weak from the beginning of the first "T" to that of the second "T" in "STATES."

In reconstructing the counterfeiting endeavors of E. Louis Smith, researchers have been supported not only by the two examples of the counterfeit postal cards glued into Smith's federal indictment, but also inadvertently by the actions of W. E. Cochran, the chief of the Bureau of the Postal Inspector from 1898 to 1904. Frank Stratton described one fabulous find in his article "The Biggest Little Counterfeiter" (February 1984, American Philatelist):

Early in 1969, I was informed by a new correspondent, Collector C, that he had uncovered a group of counterfeit cards in the stock of a New York dealer. ... The newly discovered material consisted of five items: 1. a used cover in which the other four items had been mailed; 2. a correspondence card, signed by W. E. Cochran, Chief Post Office Inspector...; 3. Three postal cards, all marked on the face with the word "Counterfeit" in red ink, in Cochran's handwriting...

Here were standards by which Smith's handiwork might be recognized. And no better authority on their "genuineness" could be asked for than from the chief inspector of the Post Office Department himself!

Two of the cards were copies of U.S. Scott #UX-14; one was addressed to E.A. Woodward in Paterson, New Jersey, but not cancelled; its reverse was uncoated and carried an ad for the Nerve Seed Remedy Co. of Chicago. The second was not addressed or cancelled; the back had a clay coating with a printed business form of the Sylvan Steel Co. of Moline, Illinois, underneath. Cochran added a short note on the reverse that explained the coating procedure for spoiled cards. The third was a mint copy of UX-12, the only mark being Cochran's red "Counterfeit" inscription.

The handwritten correspondence card from Cochran read:

W.E. Cochran
Post Office Department
Chief Post Office Inspector
Washington

April 30, 1902

Dear Mr. Terry,

    I enclose samples of the counterfeit postal cards of which you may have heard recently.

                 Sincerely yours,
                 W.E. Cochran

A fascinating question is why within days of their seizure, the chief post office inspector is sending examples of the counterfeit postal cards to this person. It is not even known if Mr. Terry was a collector. A check of the membership rolls of the American Philatelic Society does not show Mr. Terry as a member. Whatever the reason was, we are indebted to the chief inspector. These items, with the accompanying correspondence, eventually found their way into the hands of a knowledgeable stamp collector who appreciated their significance.

Out of all the bogus postal cards known to have been produced, distributed and used, very few have ever been identified in either collector or government hands. E. Louis Smith had accomplished exactly what he had intended. His cards were used, and upon receipt thrown away. If it had not been for Inspector Stuart, very possibly Smith's activities could have gone on for many more years.

It is interesting to speculate on exactly what caused Smith's downfall. It is suspected that for at least three years his bogus cards flowed through the mail. After this time of trouble-free success, just maybe he became careless. Did he begin to distribute items that previously he might have discarded as being of poorer quality? Simply put, greed and laziness may have overcome common sense and his earlier attention to detail. This would not be the last time such a mistake would spell the downfall of a criminal enterprise.

The question most frequently asked about this and every other counterfeit postal operation is why someone would go to the effort of making such a fake. Generally, the normal honest person can't understand how the criminal can make money in such an enterprise. After all, these items only sell for pennies. With E. Louis Smith they actually were sold for a penny, and he probably made an income of about $5,000 per year. The thing to remember is that in 1902 that was a very comfortable income.

Frank Stratton's research into enameled postal cards documented the legitimate purchase price paid by recyclers for misprinted cards ranged from 10 to 25 cents per 100. Many of E. Louis Smith's competitors also were selling coated cards to businesses with advertisements printed on the back at prices comparable to what Smith charged. By producing his own "originals," Smith minimized what was his competitors' main expense. Automatically, he was maximizing his profit.

If legitimate dealers in reused cards could buy their stock in trade (misprinted cards) at 10 to 25 cents per 100, coat them, and sell them at a profit, why didn't Smith do the same? A fair guess would be both greed and supply. Why pay for what you can get – or in this case, make – for almost nothing? For the other, one has to wonder just what quantity of spoiled card stock was readily available for purchase and then recycling each month. Smith, the sharp young businessman, might have reasoned, why go to the bother of searching for this raw material when with little expense or effort I could make my own in whatever quantities I need. The demand for coated cards most likely was greater than the readily available supply. Years later, other entrepreneurs would make a similar discovery in the sale of discounted postage, and even ungummed, uncancelled stamps.

The inflation of postal costs has kept counterfeiters interested in the products of the post office. Remember stamps are sold in panes, booklets, or coil rolls. You do not buy one stamp at a time, and when Smith was selling his postal cards, he also was not selling one postal card at a time. Then additionally, when the stamp counterfeiter sells his product on the street, his profit margin is actually greater for stamps than for counterfeiting $20 bills. Another consideration has to be what happens to you if by chance you get caught. The federal courts take currency counterfeiting very seriously. That same consideration is not given to postal obligations.

An unknown number of Smith's counterfeit products did elude Inspector Stuart's seizure. It is known that examples were still being identified and seized by the government as late as 1904. In the annual report for that year, the chief of the Secret Service stated that his agents had considerable activity. "There is also an item of 1013 facsimiles of United States postal cards and three altered proof postage stamps [seized]."

In the marketplace, at the 1992 Empire Colorado postal history auction, two used counterfeit U.S. postal cards, both UX-14, 1-cent Jeffersons, were offered. They are identifiable as E. Louis Smith products by the missing serif flaw. They sold for $500 each. A point of interest on these items is the fact that they do not have the enamel coating associated with Smith's previously identified work.

If you collect postal cards, you might want to take a closer look at those common early issues. Collectors now and in the future may experience the joy of making their own discovery. Even researching old cases can lead to the joy of discovery. Back when the Smith investigation first began, Captain Stuart made a statement to local reporters that for some time mystified me. In his description of Smith's arrest, Inspector Stuart commented that he believed Smith to "be connected with the stamp counterfeiters who operated recently in Lancaster, Pa." This would be determined not to be the case, but it would lead me to the rediscovery of another case, which had been heretofore totally unknown to me.

4

The Great Lancaster Counterfeit Case

"Probably the most dangerous counterfeiter schemes
ever perpetrated in the United States was conceived by
two Lancaster businessmen."

– Lancaster Historical Society

Part of the fun and mystery of research is that one never truly knows what one may discover. Digging into old news reports, time and again, one will find references to fascinating crime stories. Like following bread crumbs to a prize, every once in a while this may even lead to a new bogus stamp story. In this case, following the trail led me to Lancaster, Pennsylvania. The story found is well known to local history buffs, but not to the general public. This was a major counterfeiting case involving revenue stamps, currency, attempted bribery and collusion with government agents.

When news reports of the Lancaster counterfeiting gang did break, it was generally overlooked in the popular and philatelic press. Actually, the entire topic of bogus revenue stamps has generally been underreported. Revenue stamps are a part of the philatelic world, and just like postage stamps, postal cards and later meter impressions, they have been used as a government obligation. They also have been tageted to "enrich" those with a criminal inclination.

For me, the first hint that something had occurred in Lancaster was Captain Stuart's cryptic comment to the press. Then one day while looking for another story in the *New York Times Index*, I found a reference to the conviction of two counterfeiters in Lancaster. When I looked this case up in the Times, it told the end, not the beginning of what had been a major criminal enterprise. Trying to find other clippings was a study in frustration. Ultimately, the complete story was located in the archives of the Lancaster Historical Society. In 1979, Richard D. Shindle published a reconstruction of the events.

The public would first hear about the Jacobs Gang in the spring of 1899. What would grab attention was not that counterfeit revenue stamps were involved, but rather that this had involved official corruption and the attempted bribery of public officials. Charged as co-defendants was an ex-U.S. attorney, his law partner who had been his assistant U.S. attorney, and a deputy collector for the Internal Revenue Service. When discovery was near, it was revealed that the gang had tried to bribe agents of the Secret Service. The target of this criminal enterprise had not been just revenue stamps, but currency as well.

This was not a fly-by-night operation. The Lancaster fraud had gone on for some time. Of particular interest to the philatelic world was that these individuals had targeted the Henry Clay revenue stamp, which was applied to boxes of cigars (Springer Catalog TC146), and possibly also the issue before that one.

The masterminds of this crime were two businessmen, William M. Jacobs and William L. Kendig. Jacobs was a cigar manufacturer, and Kendig a tobacco wholesaler. Somewhere along the line they reasoned that if they did not have to pay taxes on their product, they could maximize their profit and undercut their competitors on prices. This was before the day of the income tax, and it was through excise and revenue tax stamps that the government was largely funded. Like others, they would conclude: why buy revenue stamps from the government when we can make your own?

This was not Jacobs and Kendig's first flirtation with criminal activity. The records show that in 1890, they went to New York City to purchase merchandise on credit. These items were then shipped to Philadelphia where they were re-sold at auction. When the creditors went to the New York address to collect their money, the fictitious business they operated under was no longer there. This is the same scheme that Mary Tinsey McMillan, the counterfeiter of the 1895 Chicago 2-cent Washington case, had also used before she turned to stamps.

Once the duo decided to turn to bogus revenue stamps, they determined they wanted to make a quality product. Attention to detail was paramount. To avoid detection, every effort was made to match the paper, the printing, and even the watermark that was found on the government's issue. The product they ultimately created would almost defy detection.

As with currency, the paper used for revenue stamps presented a problem. It is made to strict government specifications and is tightly controlled. The two reasoned that if they tried to buy the same security paper the government employed, questions would be asked. The answer they came up with was easy. They decided to steal it. This was not a bad idea, but they resembled the Keystone Kops in their execution. When they broke into the facility that manufactured the government's security paper, they tripped an alarm wire. Still, all was not lost. Before the authorities arrived, in the scramble to escape, they grabbed a sample of the paper they would need.

After an extensive search, Jacobs and Kendig were able to locate another paper mill, which was able to match the sample they had purloined. Then, they went further. They requested the paper they ordered have the distinctive U.S.I.R. watermark. The explanation they gave to the mill owner was that this was a secret trademark they employed for their firm, which was selling an Indian patent medicine in Europe.

Having established a source for their paper, the next step was to obtain their printing plates. To do this they went to Philadelphia. At that time Philadelphia was known as a center for quality engraving (and counterfeiting). This generated another distinguishing mark of the Lancaster case. Just like the government's product, the stamps they would produce were engraved.

In Philadelphia they soon found two individuals, Arthur Taylor and Baldwin S. Bredell, who were not only expert engravers, but individuals who were not averse to breaking the law. By early in 1896, Jacobs and Kendig had their paper and plates and were ready to begin production. It is estimated that before this scheme was discovered, these men and their revenue stamps defrauded the government of at least $125,000.

The actual printing of the revenue stamps occurred on the second floor of Kendig's tobacco warehouse, located at 212 N. Queen Street in Lancaster. This was about two blocks from the post office that also housed the government's revenue office. The printing was done by Kendig, assisted by his warehouse foreman who was an ex-policeman. Once printed, the revenue stamps were delivered to Jacobs' cigar factory, which was located adjacent to the Lancaster police station.

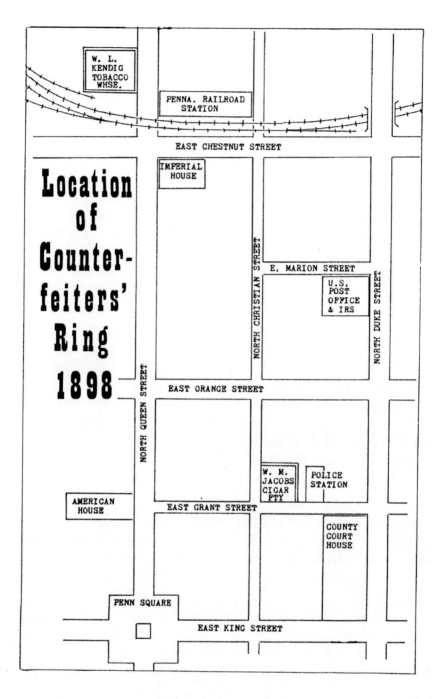

Map of Lancaster, Pa.
Courtesy of the Lancaster Historical Society

As a businessman you have to give Jacobs credit for how he merchandised his product. His selling technique was to ship out unordered boxes of cigars to tobacconists all over the country. Then, when he billed the recipients, if they objected to payment, he could always negotiate a lower sales price to complete the sale. As he was not paying any revenue tax to the government, he and his partner could always undercut the price of any of their competitors. (Does this ring a bell with E. Louis Smith in Chicago?) Everything was going fine with this scheme until they decided to branch out.

This was a fateful decision because up to this point the scheme with the revenue stamps had been working well, and had gone totally undetected. Like many stamp counterfeiters both before and after, at some point they decided to try their hand with counterfeiting currency. Again, the approach they planned to use was a creative one. Their plan was not to spend the bogus money, but rather to substitute what they produced for legitimate bills out of one of the government's sub treasuries. The idea was simple: Bribe a government cashier and make him a part of the crime.

Again, one has to give these guys credit both for originality and for thinking big. The government would later estimate the gang planned to produce at least $10 million in bogus bills. Unfortunately for the conspirators, the very complexity of what they were doing would lead to their downfall – that, and human nature.

When they set up the currency scheme, Taylor and Bredell were again called on to produce the plates, but this time they were also going to do the printing. This would lead to a very stupid decision on the printer's part. When Jacobs and Kendig did not front them the money to set up the new operation, they improvised. Unbeknown to Jacobs and Kendig, the printers used sample bills from a test printing to purchase the supplies they would need for their big press run.

When at least one of these bills was redeemed at the Philadelphia sub treasury, an alert clerk got suspicious. When he looked at this $100 silver certificate, he noticed that the color of the seal did not look quite right. Then when he began to look more closely he realized the paper also felt different. Looking further, he noticed a number of other minor discrepancies. Following the established procedure for handling suspect currency, he fired the item off to Washington for examination. It did not take the authorities long to establish that the items submitted were counterfeit.

Among the deficiencies noted was one glaring defect. When exposed to moisture, the front and back separated.[14] Still, the general consensus of the experts was that if the paper the counterfeiters used was not up to the government's standards, the printing was of a much higher quality. In fact, they thought the quality of this counterfeit was so good they immediately ordered a recall of the $100 "Monroe Head" silver certificate. This is the first and only time this has happened in the United States.

There are some lessons to be learned here. One reason people counterfeit stamps is because they are used once and thrown away. If you can get your product out into the market you have a low likelihood of discovery. When you start to play with U.S. currency, you have to know that ultimately when your product hits either a bank or the Federal Reserve, its counterfeit nature will be discovered. That is, if it even gets to the bank or the Federal Reserve. People look at money. They do not look at stamps. Another rule of thumb with currency is that the Secret Service takes this offense very seriously, and it readily commands their attention.

In this case, the counterfeit currency was promptly brought to the attention of William P. Hazen, the chief of the Secret Service. Then, when Hazen stepped down in 1898, he was replaced by John E. Wilkie. The new man in charge had originally been a crime reporter and then editor of the *Chicago Tribune*, and he firmly believed in hands-on management. He would personally direct this investigation. Supporting him as his lead field investigator was William J. Burns, who would go on to establish the detective agency that bears his name. Burns would later serve as the director of the government's Bureau of Investigation, the predecessor to the FBI.

When agents began to investigate the counterfeit currency popping up in Philadelphia, it did not take long for Taylor and Bredell to be identified as likely suspects. They were put under 24-hour surveillance. Another thing that Burns did was to trap and inspect all

---

14 One of the accomplished counterfeiters of our day used this same method. The front and the back are glued together with a computer-generated profile of Franklin sandwiched between. His artwork has driven the Secret Service nuts, and he is responsible for millions in bogus $100s. He also had the same problem with moisture. In humid climates his bills separated.

the incoming and outgoing mail and packages these two individuals either received or sent. When this is done today by postal inspectors, it is called a mail cover. This is a very secretive and controversial investigative technique, and as such is tightly controlled.[15]

Burns soon established these men had not only passed the bogus currency being identified, but they also had been acquiring all of the materials necessary to produce a large quantity of counterfeit currency. The surveillance of these subjects then paid an unexpected dividend. They were followed to Lancaster, and that is how Jacobs and Kendig were soon implicated in what was going on. First targeted for their possible involvement with the counterfeit money, it was at this point that the existence of the counterfeit revenue stamps was discovered.

On its own part the Treasury's Revenue Department had also figured out that their tax revenues were being defrauded. Aldus Herr, who had previously been a clerk at Jacobs' cigar factory, had taken a government job working for the Revenue Department. When he had been employed by Jacobs, Herr had handled both the revenue books and the tax stamps. At some point he began to put two and two together and became suspicious that something was not exactly on the up and up. Now, with his new job working for the tax man, he decided to report his suspicions to his new employer.

When Henry Hershey, the revenue collector in Lancaster, was told that his revenue was being cheated, he was incensed. He wanted something done immediately, and he promptly attempted to get a warrant to search Jacobs' business. With the Secret Service investigation now centered on both Philadelphia and Lancaster, Burns soon discovered that Hershey was moving to kick in doors and confront his suspects.

Since the Secret Service was trying to establish the guilt of these individuals, and they were not ready to make arrests, Burns pleaded with the revenue collector to wait. The goal of the Secret Service is to arrest and convict counterfeiters – not just to talk to them. Ultimately, Burns was forced to take his appeal all the way to Washington, and the Treasury Department, which oversees both of these organizations, had to intervene to hold Hershey back.

---

15 In the 1970s, one chief inspector would lose his job when Congress discovered that since World War II all mail going to communist block countries took a detour to Inspection Service offices before it was dispatched to its destination.

The investigation was not without its moments of both suspense and levity. One night, in an attempt to gather evidence, Burns and some of his agents broke into and searched Jacobs' business. It is not known if anything incriminating was found, but they were almost discovered in this endeavor. While inside the building some local residents had decided to occupy the alley to imbibe in liquid refreshments. This blocked the agents' point of exit, and they were trapped in the building until nearly dawn.

Besides Wilkie's test under fire, this was considered to be a very significant case. Lancaster was occupied by about half the total manpower of the Secret Service and every attempt was being made to remain under the radar. The agents were all operating under assumed identities. This deception almost came undone when a hotel clerk recognized Chief Wilkie from a picture that had appeared in a magazine. In spite of all their efforts, the existence of the investigation would be compromised when Samuel B. Downey, a deputy collector of revenue, tipped off Jacobs and Kendig. Downey had been on their payroll for some time, and when he discovered that his boss Henry Hershey knew of the counterfeits, he alerted the gang.

Discovering they were the target of a federal investigation, besides scrambling around to either destroy or hide any incriminating evidence, Jacobs and Kendig turned to Ellery P. Ingham for help. This individual had previously served as the United States Attorney. Besides representing these men as their attorney, he was also given the assignment of offering a bribe to one of the Secret Service agents to either kill or misdirect the government's investigation. When Jacobs approached Ingham to do this, he knew that his request would fall on receptive ears. In a previous case, Ingham had handled a $1,000 bribe to kill a case involving Jacobs. This was to secure the acquittal of two men in a perjury case. The bribe that Ingham was to pass on to the agent was not insignificant. They offered to pay the agent or agents $3,000 per month for the next two years.

It was Harvey K. Newitt, Ingham's law partner and a former assistant U.S. attorney, who presented the proposed bribe to one of the agents. This agent led him on and they thought they had a deal when money changed hands. In reality it was the criminals who were being led on, and in April of 1899, the Secret Service was finally ready to make its move. The first to be picked up were the engravers in

Philadelphia. When the print shop was searched, the agents found a partially completed plate for the duplication of "Lincoln Head" $100 bills in one desk drawer. They also found printing plates for $20 and $50 bills.

With Taylor and Bredell in custody, Chief Wilkie led his agents back to Lancaster. With a key to Kendig's tobacco warehouse they had discovered back in Philadelphia, they again made a night entry. Waiting for Kendig to arrive the next morning, they occupied their time by leisurely searching his building. When he finally walked in the door, he was taken into custody.

A treasure trove of evidence was found in the building search. There was a printing press, one plate to print the Henry Clay revenue stamps (50 impressions to a sheet), and 3,000 sheets of completed revenue stamps. Oh, and they also found nine tons of revenue quality paper. This was more revenue paper than the Bureau of Engraving and Printing kept on hand.

Wilkie and Burns personally went to Jacobs' cigar factory to take him into custody. Harvey Newitt, the attorney who was responsible for the attempted bribery of the government's agents, was arrested when he passed $500 as a payoff to one of the agents.

On Oct 20, 1899, Ingham, the ex-United States attorney, and Harvey K. Newitt, his law partner and former assistant U.S. Attorney, went on trial for conspiracy and bribery. Kendig by then had cut a deal and was put on the stand by the prosecutor. He testified that he had several meetings with Ingham and had retained him for the purpose of bribing Secret Service officers. Not surprisingly, both Ingham and Newitt were found guilty, and were sentenced to two and a half years in prison.

In June 1900, Jacobs, Kendig and the engravers were each fined $5,000 and sentenced to 12 years. The engravers, Taylor and Bredell, then had an additional seven years added to their sentences when Taylor's brother was caught spending $20 bills which they had produced and he had pocketed. These sentences had to rank among the harshest ever handed down on a case that involved the counterfeiting of stamps.[16]

---

16 Rules to remember here: Do not counterfeit currency–the government takes this very seriously. Then, do not spend your own product. The government has a great track record in tracking it back. Finally, if the jig is up, do not try to bribe the Secret Service. This generally does not work out well.

The counterfeit revenue stamps produced by Taylor and Bredell are not easily identifiable. The principle difference in design is in the shading around the head of Clay. The paper is a lighter blue and the lettering in the watermark is closer together than found in the genuine Clay revenue stamp.

Even after the gang was broken up, a number of the counterfeit items remained on the market. Many of these items are easy to identify. Just look for the rubber stamp surcharge "counterfeit" placed there by the inspector of seized cigars. Then again, to add challenge to your life, a number of these items are still out there that are not so marked. Look carefully at your revenue stamps.

The counterfeiting of revenue stamps has been one of the more unreported sides of stamp counterfeiting. If few people look at regular issue postage stamps, just how many do you think look at revenue stamps?

It was after I discovered the Lancaster case that in my research I encountered others. Remember the letter during the Civil War reporting counterfeit stamps? Totally unrelated, but in the same time frame, I found the following:

First Issue Revenue Counterfeits

In *Revenue Stamps of the United States* edited by Roger W. Sargent, I found the following material. In the chapter on first issue counterfeits three stamps are identified that have been duplicated:

1) The 1-cent Proprietary stamp of the first issue.
2) The $3 Manifest stamp of the first issue
3) The 1-cent B&HD Howard (blue) match stamp.

Amazingly, in the correspondence quoted it then goes on and identifies a fourth item.

The letter in question was from Mr. Jos. R. Carpenter at Washington D.C., dated Nov 6, 1869:

It is with much regret I enclose to you a counterfeit 1c proprietary stamp which you will please show to Mr. Earle and take care of until my return. I have also seen an excellent counterfeit of the $3.00 manifest stamp. Lathework and all well done: too well done. The public would be readily deceived by it. You doubtless saw in the papers an account of the arrest of a powerful ring of counterfeiters. The dies, rolls, and plates are secured. They confined themselves not only to stamps but engraved Government bonds and checks.

The lettering is admirable. In the 60c Tobacco stamp the counterfeit is almost as good as the original. Lathework imitated by hand admirably. The upshot of this will be that I must prepare new stamps of all the government dies.

Please send me at once a proof in the printed color (green) of the $3.00 manifest stamp, also one or two of the 1c Proprietary die in the rose pink and one or two in black.

I have been permitted to examine counterfeit plates and impressions which are enough to make me sick to see how successfully they have been done.

A little abbreviated background to the above correspondence was found in the Nov 5, 1869 edition of the *N.Y. Tribune*:

LARGE HAUL OF COUNTERFEITS

Some two months ago counterfeit tobacco stamps appeared in the market, and investigation showed that a large number had been put in circulation.

Pearce at first stoutly denied the charges, but when there was discovered, still warm in his pocket, a counterfeit $3 revenue stamp plate, he made a full confession to his captors.

After a foot & half of earth had been removed, the officers discovered a large tin box, which upon being opened was found to contain 10,500 counterfeit Rev. Stamps in large sheets, the plates for printing dies, rolls & every denomination of stamps from one cent to $80.

Some Politically Incorrect Thoughts on Revenue Tax Stamps

When you do the same thing over and over and expect different results, that is the definition of insanity. In 1919, trying to protect the public from the evils of alcohol, we passed prohibition. Criminals stepped in to supply what the public wanted. Some of the more sophisticated would even put counterfeit revenue tax stamps on their product.

Today we are doing the same thing with tobacco. When the tax stamps represent 75 percent of the product price, you have created an economic incentive. Someone somewhere is going to grasp this opportunity. It is suspected that millions in federal and state tax revenue has been lost through counterfeit revenue stamps.

One example on how tax revenue can be stolen is with gasoline. In one story I know, New York organized crime did not print stamps, they just exploited the bureaucracy. A petroleum distribution business was set up. They delivered the product and simply pocketed the state and federal gas tax. By the time the authorities visited this business address to collect the tax, they had set up business at a new address. This went on for years, to the tune of $8 million per week.

People, I think we have a problem.

5

The Deluge Begins

Between 1916 and 1923, a series of stamp cases sprang up. Perhaps this was an idea whose time had come. Some of these were amateurish events. Others very definitely were not.

St. Louis, 1916
Just Whom Can You Trust?

A stamp story appeared in the October 23, 1916 edition of the *St. Louis Post Dispatch*. The headline read: "2 years for man in counterfeiting plot / Saloon keeper who conspired to make postage stamps also fined $1,000." Thus ended what had obviously been a successful and secret investigation. The first inkling that either the press or the public had of this crime was by chance. One of the defendants forced a trial and the judge expressed his anger in the courtroom.[17]

This St. Louis criminal enterprise began on April 19, 1916, when Henry A. Howard got together with some people he trusted. He had concluded that postal revenue was ripe for exploitation. To execute this plan he recruited Roy Jones, George Watson, and Willard F. Smith. The plan he presented was to counterfeit the then current 2-cent postage stamp, which was in general use.

George Watson, who was a saloon owner in Centralia, Illinois, became the self-appointed leader of the gang. With Howard he fleshed the idea out and actively recruited the crew they would need. Then Watson organized the work of actually counterfeiting the postage stamps. The enterprise was put on a tight schedule, but as it turned out, so was the government.

---

17 One of the reasons so little is known about stamp counterfeiting is because frequently these cases never go to trial. Both the Secret Service and the Postal Inspectors maintain a conviction rate that would be the envy of most police states. When they grab you, your best bet is to plead guilty. Unfortunately, this does not produce a paper trail that is easily found.

As the plot would be described in the news reports, Smith, who owned and operated a printing shop, had been recruited to print the stamps. Howard and Jones were given the assignment of acquiring the necessary supplies and any additional equipment that would be needed. They were instructed to use assumed names so that any trail they left would be a dead end for authorities.

It did not take the gang members long to complete their assignments. The record showed that the day after the conspiracy went into motion, Howard purchased zinc plates from the National Steel and Copper Company. He also acquired printing acids from the Mayer Brothers Drug Company. These would be used to produce the printing plates. Willard Smith had the responsibility of printing the stamps, but he was not an engraver. He had the additional assignment of finding an engraver who would produce the plates used to print the stamps.

Another contribution that Smith made was the round-hole perforating machine. Smith knew where such a machine could be found and seven days into the plot, Howard and Jones went there to complete the purchase and pick it up. Other than getting the finished printing plates, the perforator would be the last item the gang would need to complete their scheme. It was also the crucial item the government would need for an eventual prosecution. Getting a round-hole perforator clearly demonstrated the criminal intent of the gang to produce the counterfeit stamps. Let's face it, there are not a lot of uses out there for round-hole perforators.

Before the production of the stamps could even begin, the criminals' plans went very wrong. Not even one bogus stamp had come off the press when government agents moved in. On April 27, Special Agent Stephen A. Connell of the Secret Service had gone before a U.S. commissioner, filed an affidavit, and obtained a warrant to arrest Howard, Jones, and Smith. A separate warrant was issued for the arrest of Watson. All the suspects were taken into custody, and the bond on each was set at $3,000. The normal contingent of crime reporters who follow the daily activities of law enforcement either completely missed the story of the arrests, or did not consider the incident of enough significance to be newsworthy. Up to this point no reports of this case had appeared in the press.

On June 12, Jones and Howard appeared in federal court to answer the charges against them. They entered guilty pleas and were promptly sentenced – Howard, to Fort Leavenworth Penitentiary for 18 months, and Jones to the St. Charles Jail for six months. Again, no mention of this court activity appeared in the local newspapers.

Watson, who had been identified as the mastermind of the enterprise, didn't believe the government had a case against him. He had committed none of the overt acts in the conspiracy. All he had done was talk to some people. He felt he could beat the government, and he defied the prosecutor to take him to trial. The government was more than willing to do that. We are indebted to this fellow's cocky attitude and his faulty reasoning. If he had not forced a public trial, and then made the judge mad, the story of this particular counterfeit plot would have disappeared into the files of the Secret Service. Once there most likely it never would have seen the light of day.

Still, there is not much of a record. On October 23, 1916, Watson's trial began, and it ended almost immediately. After the first witness was called and gave his testimony, Watson must have had second thoughts. The witness was Willard Smith, one of Watson's co-conspirators.

In the report that was finally published in the *St. Louis Post*, Smith testified that Watson had approached him about a year earlier proposing they print $100,000 worth of bogus 2-cent stamps. Agreeing to conspire, the witness described how he had been assigned to engage an engraver who would make the plates. The stamps were to be produced in Smith's printing shop and would be perforated on a machine that Smith had located. The distribution of the stamps was to be handled by Howard. Their plan was to sell the items in Chicago, not St. Louis.

When these events were described in detail, not much more testimony would have been needed to establish the government's case. Watson realized that he had seriously misjudged the government's case against him, and he moved to stop the trial. At his request his attorney immediately entered a guilty plea on his behalf. Unsurprisingly, Judge Dyer, the federal judge who was hearing this case, was not pleased.

Call it human nature, but judges from the dawn of time have felt they are overworked. Every day they look at the unending cases filling their docket. From the bench, Judge Dyer sharply informed the defendant he had no sympathy for someone who, knowing his own guilt, would admit it only after convincing evidence of his guilt had been presented. In short order Watson was fined $1,000 and sentenced to spend the next two years in custody at the Fort Leavenworth Penitentiary. It was apparent the judge's angry outburst woke up and captured the attention of the court reporters.

As soon as the case against Watson was over, Smith again was brought before Judge Dyer. This time it was as a defendant and he entered a guilty plea. Accepting his plea, the judge closed the case by fining Smith one dollar.

Following the usual policy of the Secret Service, the method they employed to first uncover and then terminate this scheme was never revealed. One possibility is that the printer, Smith, after being approached about becoming a member of this criminal enterprise, had second thoughts and went to the authorities. Another possibility is that Smith, for one reason or another, was already an informant for the authorities. The Secret Service has always kept voluminous records on those who like to duplicate the government's products. They also track various printing supplies and equipment a counterfeiter would use. To this day, if you try to recruit a printer or engraver to help in a counterfeiting enterprise, you should not be surprised if your contact turns out to be a Secret Service informant, or even an agent himself.

After examining the public record one can only conclude that, from the gang's point of view, the wrong person had been recruited. Special Agent Connell knew as much about what was going on as the conspirators did. He never let the gang get to the point where they could actually produce the stamps. The first physical act that would substantiate their criminal intent was the purchase of the perforating machine. This occurred on April 25, and on April 27 the Secret Service filed the affidavit to obtain the arrest warrants. The only way this could have occurred was if one member of the group had been acting as an informant for the government.

If this trial had gone to its conclusion the government had been well prepared. Willard Smith may have been the primary witness, but he was not the only arrow the government had in their quiver. In the margin of the original court documents someone had written the names of four witnesses the government planned to call. Besides Smith, the others would have testified to the sale of plates, acids and the perforating machine. Emphasizing the importance of Smith to the government's case, the prosecution had listed Smith's name again at the bottom of the list and circled it twice.

Sometimes a person just doesn't know whom they can trust.

Minneapolis, 1919
A Stamp Known for Its Taste

One day I was reading an old philatelic newspaper when the following item caught my eye. It was in the August 23, 1919, edition of *Mekeel's Weekly Stamp News*:

> Forged – is a poor watermark better than none? Mr. Ragatz sends a clipping: Minneapolis, Aug 9. – An alleged counterfeiter of stamps, K.C. Brewer, was arrested by the federal officer after the Minneapolis detectives had detained him as a result of Brewer's possession of a number of counterfeit stamps and an engravers outfit, alleged to belong to him." Assuming that the current U.S. were the object of attention, it is recalled that it was a stamp counterfeiting case that was responsible for the adoption of the watermark in the 1895 issue.

There's that watermarked paper myth again. It is a glaring example on how urban legends are created and established in the public mindset.

When this brief note was found in *Mekeel's,* the next step was to go to the Minnesota Historical Society. After reading a month's worth of old newspapers, a few brief but pertinent references were found. Looking for the court record a scant criminal file was found. When the local information sources were exhausted the next step was to check the Kansas Federal Archives. Their records consisted of a docket sheet and a one page indictment. From these bits and pieces the outline of a story was pieced together.

On the night of August 8, 1919, Frank C. Brewer (not K.C., as cited in *Mekeel's*) was arrested in the room he was renting at 100 Thirteenth Street in Minneapolis. Detectives Frank Brunskill and

Walter Bryant of the Minneapolis Police Department made the arrest. The newspaper account stated Brewer was an engraver, and when the detectives entered his lodging they reportedly found him in the act of actually "making counterfeit two-cent stamps." While searching his room the officers found a number of the spurious stamps together with the plates, paper and inks he used in making the bogus items. All of this material was seized by the officers, and Brewer was taken into custody. Because he had allegedly printed and sold counterfeit stamps, Brewer was held until he could be turned over to the federal authorities.

It was reported that what tripped up this faker was the tongue test. As the *Minneapolis Journal* would headline the story, "Stamps Taste Wrong." In the story, the strange-flavored mucilage was noticed by those who purchased and used Brewer's stamps. This was commented on to postal employees who in turn brought it to the attention of the inspectors. Once alerted, the postal inspectors began the tedious job of identifying the seller. They would have brought in the Minneapolis detectives to assist them in the investigation. For reasons not stated, the detectives soon suspected Brewer was the source.

One of the great strengths of the Postal Inspection Service has always been its ability to work with local law enforcement, or as I like to describe it, we play well with others be they federal or local. Chief inspectors long ago recognized there were a great many more local police than inspectors. When agencies and departments work together, there can be good results. Treated as equals, local police become the eyes and ears of the field inspector. In turn they get the total support of postal authorities. This philosophy worked well in this case.

The day after Brewer's arrest, the inspectors took him before the U. S. commissioner. Postal Inspector R.N. Hugdahl and Police Detective Walter Bryant testified, presenting stamps, plates, paper and ink as evidence. According to the *Minneapolis Tribune,* Inspector Hugdahl asserted that "the plates and paraphernalia seized were of the kind only used by the government printing office." Obviously Inspector Hugdahl had never visited the Bureau of Engraving and Printing. The government's printing equipment would hardly fit into a suitcase. Bail was set at $3,000 and Brewer was remanded to the county jail.

The court documents show that on October 7, 1919, this case was presented to a Federal Grand Jury. Not surprisingly they quickly returned an indictment charging Brewer with two counts:

1. Counterfeiting certain plate and die for forging and counterfeiting 2-cent postage stamps.

2. Having in his possession, with the intent to use, a certain counterfeit die and plate for the forging and counterfeiting of 2-cent United States postage stamps.

On October 9, Brewer entered a plea of not guilty, but then on October 17, the case was "Nolled" (i.e., Nolle Prosequi, "to be unwilling to pursue"). This is an entry of record signifying the plaintiff or prosecutor will not press a charge in a given case. With the October 17 court entry, this case completely drops off the map. Now I have no idea how rigorously search and seizure laws were interpreted in 1919, but just maybe when the door to Brewer's lodgings was kicked in, the detectives lacked a critical element – a search warrant. The entire case against Brewer seems to have been haphazard at best. The one thing that was missing appears to have been an investigation, and if the search was challenged, there would be nothing for the prosecution to fall back on. Other than that suspicion, I have no idea why this prosecution was dropped.

No information was ever found on how many stamps Brewer may have made and sold before his activities were interrupted in Minnesota. One really cannot come down hard on either the inspectors or the detectives for the paucity of an investigation. It appears that before his arrest, Brewer had only been in the Twin Cities for about 10 days. It was reported he had just recently arrived from Seattle. Discovering his criminal activity, it was a lot easier for the authorities to just give him a train ticket and get him out of their jurisdiction. This is not an unknown event in the annals of law enforcement. Now if Brewer had been a little more familiar with the area, he might have moved his operation across the river to St. Paul. There, for the payment of a small fee to the chief of police, he could have operated with impunity.

Minnesota today has a reputation for being squeaky clean. That was not the case in the early 20th century. St. Paul was a mecca for criminals who came from all over the country. Other than making your contribution to the chief of police's retirement fund, the only requirement was that you did not practice your profession within the city limits. This was a system that worked for years until prominent citizens began to be kidnapped and held for ransom.

Nothing is known about Brewer's history on the West Coast, but one can imagine that his Minneapolis enterprise was not a new endeavor. Forced to leave Minnesota one can only wonder what happened to him next. Counterfeiting, be it of currency or of stamps, is not a crime of impulse. Criminals tend to have career "specialties." This is especially true of counterfeiters. They do not suddenly decide to start robbing banks. One can only presume that wherever Brewer next set up shop most likely he resumed the activity in which he was proficient. Maybe he even purchased a better brand of mucilage.

Brewer's career and ultimate fate were not the only mysteries remaining at the end of my research into this case. While looking for information on Brewer, another discovery was noted. In the August 17, 1919, edition of the *Minneapolis Sunday Tribune* the following comment was noted: "This is the first case of alleged stamp counterfeiting heard here for several years." A simple question arises: If this was the first in some time, just when, what and where were the previous ones?

Similarly, in the October 18, 1919, issue of *Mekeel's* the following tidbit appeared: "Mr. Percy M. Mann mentioned to your editor that he had heard of counterfeit postage stamps having been recently found in Milwaukee, but we have been unable to learn any of the details." Neither have I, and to my knowledge, neither has anyone else.

Both the St. Louis case and the Brewer case in St. Paul then vanished without a trace. One can only speculate how many other events such as this have also occurred. It is my suspicion that this has been a common occurrence in the past.

Berlin, 1920
I Will Take My Business Elsewhere

In an effort to help finance America's entry into World War One, in 1917 the Treasury Department began to issue War Savings Stamps. With a face value of first 25 cents and then of $5 it would not be long before counterfeiters turned their attention to these items.

In October of 1919, reports began to surface first in Newark and then in Philadelphia that what appeared to be counterfeit War Savings Stamps were being found. It is known that on the East Coast, Secret Service agents identified and then seized several thousand dollars' worth of these bogus stamps. No arrests are known to have been made, nor could any final dispositions of any of these investigations be found.

In an event that most likely was totally unrelated to the aforementioned, an interesting twist to the War Savings Stamps appeared. In April of 1920, a person who claimed to be a resident of Pleasant Grove, Utah, was arrested in Germany. Police authorities in Berlin released information they had discovered and then broken up a plot to counterfeit both U.S. currency and postage stamps. It is not known what postage stamps were targeted, but a plan to duplicate War Savings Stamps was in the works.

In many foreign countries law enforcement can be much more intrusive than in the United States. When you have very proactive investigators, information finds its way to the ears of authorities. The police were hearing that a foreigner was attempting to get high-quality engraving work done by legitimate German firms. Specifically what he was requesting were plates that would duplicate both United States currency and stamps. It did not take a great deal of deductive reasoning to conclude that someone had criminal intent.

What happened next is universal to police across the globe. They set up surveillance and a sting. From the point of view of any criminal perpetrator if they have two brain cells to rub together they are subject to paranoia. They are always looking for a trap. Suspecting he was walking into a police trap, when it became time to pick up the completed plates the mysterious "foreigner" did not show up. Still, the Berlin police did not give up. They transmitted a warning to other jurisdictions.

It did not take long to get results. It was discovered that another order for printing plates had been placed with a shop in Liegnitz, Silesia. The firm in Liegnitz had determined what was being requested was beyond their capabilities. Still not wanting to lose the order, they subcontracted it to another company, which was located in Berlin. When this was discovered, the police commissioner instructed the Berlin firm to go ahead and complete the order and then ship the item to Silesia. The plates that had been ordered were for the printing of the $5 U.S. War Savings Stamp (Scott #WS4, issued July 3, 1919).

In Silesia the police set up a new surveillance and this time on the appointed date a man who they would identify as Philip Kopp attempted to pick up his order. He carefully inspected the work that had been done and, satisfied, handed over 25,000 marks for the completed printing plates. It was at this point the police agents who were waiting in the shop identified themselves and Kopp was taken into custody.

Not surprisingly, Kopp protested that he was innocent of any criminal activity. He explained to the officers he was a legitimate businessman visiting from Pleasant Grove, Utah. His story was that back in the United States he owned a number of fruit stores, and he was acquiring the printing plates not to print counterfeit stamps, but rather for "advertising purposes." On the $5 War Savings Stamps made from these plates he planned to carry the legend, "Buy your fruit only at Philip Kopp's stores." Right.

Police the world over are noted for their cynicism. If the lay person day after day had to hear the bizarre and improbable presented as explanations for a particular conduct, most likely a similar life view would soon develop. Needless to say Kopp's alibi was received with more than a little skepticism.

Whatever the ultimate fate was for Kopp is unknown as all further news of this case dropped out of the public's view. For that matter, it is not even known if this was the true identity of the individual in question. It does, however, show us an imaginative way to obtain the tools necessary for a first-class counterfeiting operation.

You might ask why the mysterious Mr. Kopp would go to

Germany to get his counterfeit plates made. Considering that Germany had just recently been pounded into the ground in the war, he may have figured, if they catch me what will they do? Not a lot of love was lost between Germany and the Allies, and he surely would not need to worry about the U.S. Secret Service. Then again the quality of the work that could be done by master engravers would be excellent. The workmanship of German engravers was more than demonstrated at the end of World War II. Millions in English £5 notes that virtually defied detection were discovered at the bottom of a Bavarian lake.

More Battles with War Savings Stamps

After the government created the War Savings Stamp, Philip Kopp was not the only one who sensed a business opportunity. Other individuals would not go to Germany to perpetrate their crime. In the *San Francisco Chronicle* the following appeared.[18]

> A government employee in examining some war savings stamps presented for redemption discovered the toothache. He had seen many of the Government's engravings of Franklin and the fact of a pronounced swelling on one cheek struck him as a recent development. Further examination proved that it was a counterfeit toothache.

This certainly was the same counterfeit 1919 War Savings Stamp the Postmaster General was issuing a warning notice about in the May 1920 *Official Postal Guide*, Notice 36. It is described as follows:

(36) COUNTERFEIT 1919 WAR SAVINGS STAMP

1. A very dangerous counterfeit of the blue war savings stamp, series 1919, has been discovered.

2. It is printed from a steel plate on a good grade of paper, and is a close reproduction of the genuine. There are a number of defects, however, some of which are as follows:

---

18 The date of the Chronicle article is not known but it was reproduced in the June 5, 1920 issue of Mekeel's Weekly Stamp News.

The left cheek of Franklin has a pronounced swelling. The lower one of the two left dots below the portrait is comparatively indistinct. The vertical opening between the lines in the lower left part of the numeral "2" in "1924" is closed.

3. The swelling in the cheek of Franklin is the most marked defect. Most of the other differences are so slight that expert examination is required to detect them.

4. The Chief of the Secret Service, Treasury Department, will send specimens of the counterfeit, so far as they are available, to Secret Service operatives throughout the country, together with a known genuine 1919 war savings stamp.

5. Postmasters are directed to select an officer or employee of known exceptional abilities and judgment, and have him acquaint himself with the characteristics of the counterfeit as described in paragraph 2 hereof.

6. When application is made for payment of 1919 war-savings certificates, the applicant should be notified to present the certificates promptly for examination, with the statement that this step is necessary because of the existence of a dangerous counterfeit.

7. An interim receipt should be given the applicant to be taken up later on payment. Each certificate should be marked plainly with the name and address of applicant. The stamps should be examined carefully by the officer or employee selected as instructed in paragraph 5 hereof.

8. A certificate may contain both genuine and counterfeit stamps. Careful examination should therefore be made of each stamp.

9. If the stamps are undoubtedly genuine, the certificate should be paid on expiration of the 10 days' notice, provided the application otherwise conforms to regulation on the subject.

10. If doubt of the genuineness of the stamps exists, they should be sent promptly by registered mail with a statement of the facts to the Post Office inspector in charge, who will submit them to the nearest Secret Service operative.

11. It is not necessary to make examination of 1919 war savings stamps registered before January 1, 1920, as the counterfeit was issued after that date.

Hard on the heels of this first discovery, another bogus item appeared on the scene. This report was found in the very next issue of the Official Postal Guide:

(35) COUNTERFEIT 1919 WAR SAVINGS STAMP

1. Another dangerous counterfeit of the blue war savings stamp, series 1919, in addition to the one which caused the issuance of Notice No. 34, May *Postal Guide*, has been discovered.

2. It is printed from a steel plate on a good grade of white paper, and is a close reproduction of the genuine. There are several defects, however, some of which are as follows:

> The counterfeit is a somewhat lighter shade of blue than the genuine stamp, and the printing is found under a magnifying glass to be not so distinct.

> The hyphen in the words "War-Savings" at the top looks more like a period than a hyphen.

> A distinct white vertical line appears in the counterfeit along the edge of Franklin's left cheek.

> The upper little ball or dot between the laurel leaves on the righthand side of the stamp, at the left of the August price "4.19," is not so distinct as in the original, and looks more like a part of the leaf.

3. The white vertical line near the edge of Franklin's left cheek is the most marked defect. Most of the other differences are so slight that expert examination will be required to detect them.

4. The Chief of the Secret Service, Treasury Department, will send photographic enlargements of the counterfeit stamp, and also of the genuine for comparison, to secret service operatives throughout the country, and post office inspectors will be provided with such photographs.

5. Postmasters are directed to examine with great care all 1919 war savings stamps presented for payment or for registration, with a view to detecting counterfeits described in this notice, and they shall be governed by the provisions of paragraph 5 to 10 of No.36, May Postal Guide.

War savings stamps, series 1919, shall be registered until their genuineness is confirmed by careful examination.

Once again a mystery is presented. Was this one plant putting out two very high- quality bogus items, or could this have been two different operations where different individuals identified a business opportunity? Judging from the warning notices by the government, it is suspected these items were available and were actively used to defraud the government. If the philatelic world missed the message, apparently the government did not. A little note was found on page 25 of the May 7, 1920, edition of the *New York Times:*

Will Stop Cashing Bad War Stamps

WASHINGTON, May 6 – After Chairman Good of the Appropriations Committee had told of two new counterfeit war stamps, the House unanimously adopted today an amendment to the pending Sundry Civil bill appropriating $50,000 to build up an organization to prevent cashing of the spurious stamps. Experts will be stationed in all large cities to protect Postmasters from redeeming the counterfeit stamps.

Let me throw out another idea here. My suspicion is this is an example of "organized crime" getting involved in the stamp trade. Distribution was on both the East and the West Coast. This was either two separate and very good operations, or one very big one. To find the answer one would have to get into the files of the Secret Service. In response to my inquiries, I was told no records could be found. We know these stamps were printed and distributed. We have no idea how many stamps were found by the government, or if anyone was ever arrested.

Questions, Questions, Questions ...

West Allenhurst, New Jersey, 1921
New York, New York, 1922-23
Who Made the Stamps?

The 1920s were anything but innocent. Crime in the United States was both exploding and changing. Besides the lone wolf, you had gangs forming primarily along ethnic lines. Ultimately, the end result we would give a name – organized crime. Not surprisingly, they would look on both the Treasury Department and the Post Office as targets of opportunity. A major center for this activity would be New York City.

In the annals of postal counterfeiting, the period of 1921-23 was challenging. Not just one, but a number of counterfeiting operations would be discovered. In New York, one was reportedly a masterful enterprise that never has been officially solved. Another was soon identified and reportedly smashed before it got off the ground. Then again, maybe it didn't. Both of these cases demonstrated a growing interest from established criminal elements in reproducing Treasury and postal products. Finally, another case was found which dwarfed everything that had gone before.

The War Savings Stamps that had been discovered in 1919 were obviously not the product of any amateur operation. The plate work and printing was of a superior quality. Then, to bring these items into your local post office and sell the bogus item back to the government was the height of audacity. Add to that the fact that distribution appears to have been nationwide and you have a very strong indication that this was not some back room mom and pop operation. Both production and distribution had been well thought out.

When I tried to follow the trail of the War Savings Stamps, I was once again led down a rabbit hole. In October 1921 a major counterfeiting operation involving millions of dollars was broken up. The report said the Secret Service had raided a bungalow in West

Allenhurst, New Jersey and arrested five men. It was reported that "a vast quantity of postage stamps of every denomination" had been found. West Allenhurst was in northern New Jersey, on a rail line leading to New York City. It did not take a major jump in deductive reasoning to say – Ah, print in the country, distribute in the city.

The report in *Mekeel's* was fairly extensive:

> Five men were arrested recently in West Allenhurst, New Jersey, after secret service agents had raided a bungalow there and seized a vast quantity of counterfeit stamps of every denomination. Close watch kept by secret service men on the movements of Giles M. Ranney, alias "Davidson," led to the raiding of the bungalow and the arrest of Ranney and four other alleged confederates.

> According to government agents, several weeks before one of the five men went into a drugstore in New York and asked to purchase a certain kind of acid. The druggist told the man that he had none in stock. When he left the druggist promptly communicated with detectives, being of the opinion that the acid for which the men asked was the sort used by counterfeiters.

> The police turned the case over to the Secret Service, and the man who sought to purchase the acid was arrested, but released. The government agents did not lose track of him, however. One of the men assigned to watch him followed him to West Allenhurst, and it was then the authorities became aware of the extent of the counterfeiter's operations.

> Huge quantities of bogus stamps had been turned out at the West Allenhurst plant, it was said, and the distribution of them was to begin immediately. All stamps manufactured were seized by the raiders, who also took charge of a complete set of counterfeiting machinery.

> The counterfeiters, it was said, had also planned to manufacture some of their bogus stamps in New York, and had made elaborate arrangements for the distribution of their product there.

The only problem with this dramatic and interesting story is that not surprisingly it is largely inaccurate. Digging into contemporary local newspapers, I discovered there were many more details about what occurred in West Allenhurst. The first report of this stamp fraud appeared in the *New York Times* in the October 16, 1921, edition, and

John S. Tucker, who was the agent in charge of the New York office of the Secret Service, was the source of the information.

The report stated that in June, Agent Tucker had received information from a druggist near Sherman Square that certain men had given him an "enormous order" for a type of chemical that would commonly be used in the manufacturing of printing plates. The druggist had direct knowledge of this sort of activity as chemicals used in a previous counterfeiting case had been traced back to him with painful results. Learning from that incident, the druggist stalled the man and promptly contacted Agent Tucker.[19]

Secret Service agents were immediately dispatched to the drugstore, and when the chemicals were ready for delivery, the "druggist's clerk" who made the delivery was in fact a Secret Service agent. The chemicals were delivered to an apartment on West 76 Street near Riverside Drive, where the man called "Ramy" accepted them. A surveillance of the apartment was set up, and five suspects were singled out and identified as members of the conspiracy.

Movements of the gang were not limited to New York City. Secret Service agents followed members of the gang to West Allenhurst, New Jersey, where it was found they had rented a "palatial residence." This building was big enough to accommodate all five members of the gang for the summer, and two of their significant others. The agents spent July and August watching the comings and goings at this house.

The *Times* observed the agents saw "that enough paper was being moved into the house to supply a fair-sized printing plant." Then in September when the gang moved back to New York City, the next day agents moved in. They searched the building and found what they were looking for in the cellar. Left behind were "many scraps of paper, broken engraving plates, some torn $5 War Savings Stamps, some torn postage stamps and other debris that showed the Treasury watch dogs just what sort of a game the men they were watching were up to."

Back in Manhattan, the agents discovered the gang was now experimenting with copying corporate securities. William Butler,

---

19 This is a common investigation technique of field agents. Chicago, for example, is a hub for printing equipment and supplies. Businesses that deal in used printing equipment are visited regularly. Of course one way around this is to bypass the supply houses and just visit local printers. You can usually find whatever you need gathering dust in the basement.

who the *Times* said "apparently took the initiative in all the activities of the gang," had established a connection with an employee of a Wall Street financial house. They hatched a scheme to get away with $75,000 in legitimate securities by substituting counterfeit copies into the brokerage account of an elderly woman. To accomplish this, one bond had been taken from the security firm's vault and used to make a plate from which copies could be printed. The newspaper reported that counterfeit War Savings Stamps and postage stamps which ranged "from 5-cents to $1 denomination" were also going to be printed and sold through "fences."

On October 15, 1921, the government was ready to make its move and they raided a Broadway hotel, where "a large quantity of counterfeit securities, plates and engravings, and other articles used in counterfeiting" were seized. The *Times* reported that "none of the counterfeited securities had been put into circulation, as the plotters were nabbed just as they had perfected their counterfeits and were about to spring their scheme." Nothing was said in the press report about the seizure of postage stamps, though an unknown quantity and variety of stamps obviously had been produced. There is no question this was a sizable conspiracy being executed by professional criminals. The *Times* article reported that one of the prisoners told the authorities the gang had expected to make $1,000,000 from their counterfeiting operation. It seems reasonable to conclude they had already been distributed and put on the market.

In custody, the suspects were identified in the *Times* as follows:

> Giles M. Rammey or Ramy, alias Fred Thomas, had been released from the Atlanta Federal Penitentiary two years earlier after serving five years for passing counterfeit $10 bills in Joplin, Missouri.
>
> William Butler, alias Bennet, age 39, was dubbed "the brains" of the gang by the Times. He had previously served time in the Atlanta Federal Penitentiary. His crime was impersonating a government official and extortion of $60,000 from a woman. It is believed Rammey and Butler hatched the counterfeiting scheme while both were incarcerated in Atlanta.[20]

---

20   This would not be the last time this happened. In the 1980s I had one counterfeiter relate to me how he had honed his printing skills while working in the prison printing shop. Another one actually ordered his printing supplies for delivery to his residence while still incarcerated.

J. Grayson Banner, alias Young, age 33.

William Neely, alias Bick, age 29.

Also arrested was Guy Pflum, age 23, who was last arrested in September 1921 on the complaint of Sailing W. Baruch (the brother of Bernard M. Baruch). Pflum had been charged with attempting to extort money from Sailing Baruch by blackmail, and could well have been Butler's connection to the world of Wall Street. He also was the likely source of the idea of substituting counterfeits for good securities in customers' accounts.

At this point, in yet another of many frustrating moments, the West Allenhurst case drops from sight. On December 23, 1922, one Giles M. Rammey, who, according to the *New York Times* was "an expert photoengraver," came into view again. Detectives for the American Express Company, assisted by operatives of the Burns International Detective Agency, arrested Rammey in Asbury Park, New Jersey. The charge this time was making fraudulent American Express travelers' checks, $15,000 of which were in his possession when arrested.

Rammey's federal prison records in Atlanta and Galveston were cited by the newspapers, though no mention was made of his October 1921 counterfeiting escapade. On February 26, 1923, Rammey entered a guilty plea in the New Jersey State Court to the charge of counterfeiting travelers' checks and was sentenced to serve three years in the state prison. That dissolved Rammey's later scheme, but all attempts to locate the disposition of the West Allenhurst case ran into a brick wall. The New York City Police Department referred me to the Secret Service. The Secret Service claimed they could locate no information on this offense. At the National Archives, the response was, "Sorry, the case in New Jersey was not adequately recorded." The search goes on to find out what truly happened here.

Another mystery started innocently enough. On page 32 of the February 3, 1922, edition of the *New York Times* there was the headline: "COUNTERFEIT 2-CENT STAMPS FOUND HERE / Dealer informs Government of Clever Forgery, First of Kind Since 1894."

The article continued:

An excellent counterfeit of the current two-cent United States postage stamp has just appeared here. A stamp dealer who is quick at detecting peculiarities in postage stamps discovered the forgery. He has several hundred of the counterfeits in his possession awaiting inspection by a Post Office Department official.

Edward Stern of the Economist Stamp Company, 87 Nassau Street, is probably the first man to detect the difference between the two-cent forgeries and the genuine issue. Early in the week, Mr. Stern said yesterday, a man interested in stamps came to his office with a few sheets of ten United States two-cent stamps, all properly gummed but a shade lighter in color than the customary deep red. Closer inspection disclosed the fact that the "U" in the word "United" on the stamp at the upper left-hand corner of the sheet of ten was imperfect at the curve. There were several other minor defects. The perforation number is twelve instead of eleven.

Mr. Stern offered to buy the stamps at their face value and when told that others might be had, asked for more. "As a result, I got several sheets of ten, numbering several hundred stamps," said Mr. Stern. "The defective "U" was clearly apparent on every sheet, showing conclusively that the stamps were printed in sheets of ten. The man who sold them to me did not know that the stamps were counterfeit, saying that the person from whom he obtained them had purchased them from a lot of unused stock from a big mail order house.

"I got the big batch of forgeries on Wednesday and immediately sent a sheet with an explanation to the United States Bureau of Printing and Engraving at Washington. I have not noticed any counterfeits on letters, nor have I heard that any collectors or dealers have found any copies, which they would doubtless detect from the lighter shade.

The counterfeits in Mr. Stern's office are very cleverly done, being executed in the surface printing style adopted by the government several years ago. They look somewhat like lithographed stamps. Mr. Stern believes the stamps have been counterfeited in sheets of ten because they would be easier to sell in small quantities in that form to merchants, as remnants purchased from large concerns. Moreover, counterfeiting is easier in small units...Inquiry at the post office here disclosed the fact that none of the officials knew of the new counterfeit."

There are moments in time when everyone in law enforcement absolutely detests the media – be it newspaper, the radio, or now, cable TV. In New York, one such moment for postal inspectors and the Secret Service must have occurred on February 3, 1922, with the publication of the Stern interview. Their investigation had just become much more difficult. Any hunter knows it is harder to track your prey when it knows it is being tracked. Just in case they missed it, Stern followed it up with another interview on February 18.

As it turned out, the story printed in the *Times* contained a number of minor errors, and under Stern's byline in the February 18 issue of *Mekeel's* he told more of the story. In this account on February 1 "a collector" came into his office with a "block" of the current 2-cent stamps. What had caught the collector's attention was that he thought he noticed these items had a peculiar shade. Stern asked if more could be obtained, and the collector said he would try. To be certain of having at least some examples, Stern persuaded the collector to part with the block of four, which "answered my purpose," he wrote.

The collector returned with several hundred stamps, all of which were in blocks of ten, at which time Stern closely inspected them and found they actually had been printed in a 10-stamps-per-sheet format. This was established by the fact that each of the stamps showed minor differences that were repeated on each sheet in the same position.

Stern wrote: "I at once notified the U.S. Secret Service Agents and sent a sheet to the Bureau of Printing and Engraving at Washington, and since that time notices have appeared in all the daily newspapers." Stern further stated that the stamps were "engraved and printed from a steel plate, and it is an imitation made to resemble the photo-process printing. ... The perforation is 11.5, and they were printed both on thin and thick paper. I fully believe that the object in working them in sheets of ten was to pass them off on mail-order houses, thus causing less suspicion than if offered in full sheets. This is the first counterfeit placed on the market since 1894."

An article by George B. Sloane in the *Collectors Club Philatelist* (April 1922) again credits the discovery of the new counterfeits to Stern and also to John A. Kleeman. Both men were identified as "well known dealers." For his part Kleeman was a respected stamp dealer and expert on U.S. stamps, so it is unlikely he was the "man interested in stamps" who had originally brought the off-colored stamps into Stern's Nassau Street office. One would suspect Kleeman would have known better, and not required any identification help from Stern. In any event, how Kleeman might have gotten involved is not known, but most likely Stern would have shared this discovery with his colleague. Kleeman himself was not unknown to controversy. Just a few years previously he had been involved with what would be known as the Hawaiian Missionary counterfeits, a great mystery still controversial to this day.

Writing in *Mekeel's*, Philip H. Ward Jr. in July of 1962, speculated that these stamps had been "printed in these small sheets, perforated and then the margins removed." Ward wrote that he had never seen one of the counterfeits with a margin or a straight edge. I have never seen a straight edge or margin either, but one day years ago while looking through a Midwest stamp dealer's box of counterfeits I did encounter a complete sheet of 10. I did not recognize the significance of what I was looking at until much later.

When Dr. David Bennett was researching the stamps of the Offset Printing Issue of 1918-20, he came upon this counterfeit. He was uncertain about his identification of exactly which stamp was being duplicated. This was clear from the title of his article in the February 1978 *United States Specialist*, Counterfeit of the 2c Stamp, Scott's #528 A(?). Bennett explained his title by saying that the 2-cent stamps he specialized in came in five distinct types, and he believed that the counterfeiter had modeled his fake after a Type VI: i.e., Scott #528A. Bennett illustrated his reconstruction of a 10-subject sheet of the fakes, but admitted that only "a few multiples and singles" had been available to work with in his research.

Dr. Bennett described the color of the fake as matching that of the genuine "rather closely," though Stern thought the color "peculiar." Slone, writing in 1922, called it "an unusually light shade." Bennett thought the color was "somewhat brighter" than the genuine because of the lack of detail lines above Washington's ear.

Bennett was most excited, however, by his belief that the counterfeits were not lithographed (surface printing or offset printing) as the genuine stamps were, but rather were engraved, "probably from a copper plate." Stern had stated in his *Mekeel's* article that the stamps "are engraved and printed from a steel plate, and it is an imitation made to resemble the photo-process printing."

Both authors were using the term "engraved" generically to mean recess printing. Bennett was probably more correct in his analysis when he wrote, "Each of the ten subjects were individually hand-etched into the soft metal plate." Bennett pointed out that the laborious process of creating each subject, one by one, would explain the small, 10-stamp format. It also would explain the differences from one stamp to another.

Ken Lawrence, an expert in U.S. Stamps, believes these fakes were made from an etched waxed copper plate. When he used a powerful expertize-quality magnifier to examine the pair of stamps that came from Dr. Bennett, Lawrence said that what Bennett identified as a "lack of sufficient lines" above the ear was plainly revealed as indistinct blobs of ink with no trace of engraved lines. These are, however, exactly the kind of ink pools that would be found in this less precise etching process. The designs do have the raised feel and appearance of intaglio printing that many collectors associate, incorrectly, only with engraving. Lawrence added that etching is not a method normally used for printing counterfeit stamps, and previous guesses that these counterfeits had been engraved were both logical and understandable.

With engraved (recess) plate printing, the impression is first cut into a soft metal plate. In the printing process, the ink is transferred to the paper under pressure and the finished product will have a raised feeling to the printing image. In typographic (relief) printing, the plate itself has the raised printing area. The impression that is transferred to the paper is indented.

In offset (surface) printing, an image is developed onto a metal plate by a photographic process. The inked image is transferred to a printing blanket that in turn transfers the impression to the surface of the paper. The entire image surface has a flat printing area. One field test used to identify most counterfeit stamps is simply to run your fingernail over the printed image. If it feels like a flat piece of paper it probably was produced by offset printing and just might be counterfeit. This field test obviously no longer works on many current issues of U.S. postage.

We are fortunate that so many philatelic experts have studied the Edward Stern stamps. It has produced a wealth of information enabling the collector to identify these items. Unfortunately, the same cannot be said for whatever investigation occurred. If any arrests were ever made, this has never been disclosed to the public. A final thought to ponder. It is significant that these items were in the hands of a big mail order house. Someone had figured out one solution to the distribution problem.

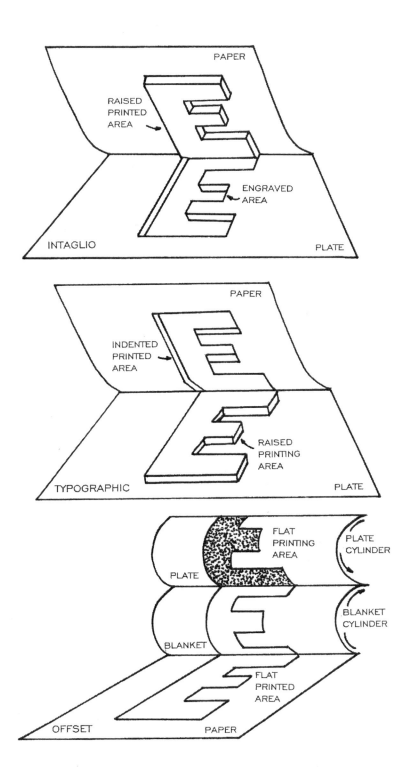

6

New York, New York, 1922-23

Booze, Bills and Counterfeit Stamps

In this country, the emergence of organized crime as a major force was largely the byproduct of good intentions gone awry. The U.S. electorate outlawed the manufacture, sale and distribution of intoxicating liquors for personal consumption. The end result was that across the nation, young immigrant boys sensed a business opportunity. People wanted booze and the law be damned. The question of who would control the supply of liquor and the wealth that came with it was arbitrated on the streets of our cities at gunpoint.

A small group of men, primarily of Italian and Sicilian descent, eventually won out. What had been just one more group of immigrants would become synonymous with the organization of criminal activity in the United States. By seizing control of the movement of illegal alcohol, this group of men became unique in the annals of U.S. criminal history. The wealth generated from bootlegging formed the catalyst that would transform the American Mafia to its position of power.

However, illegal booze was but one of many criminal enterprises the "mob," under one of its many nicknames, would turn its hand to. Counterfeiting both currency and stamps would be one of the endeavors it would explore. Since day one, be it known as the "Black Hand" or "La Cosa Nostra," organized crime was fascinated with the concept of literally "making money." It was a smaller step to try duplicating stamps.

Going back to 1900, Giuseppe Morello, the man who would be identified as the first "boss of bosses" would counterfeit currency. Time and again this would bring him to the attention of the Secret Service. Morello's adventures in printing would be sprinkled with violence and murder.

In tracing the 2-cent Washington stamps that had been identified in February of 1922, I always suspected there was a connection between the illegal trade in booze, bogus currency, and the counterfeiting of stamps. My research soon removed any doubts I had. The traditions and operations established by Giuseppe Morello were being continued.

In the October 16, 1920, edition of *Mekeel's* (p. 545), a short item appeared:

FORGED REVENUE STAMPS

BUFFALO, Oct. 8 – Arrests are expected to be made shortly by prohibition agents of members of the whiskey ring which is believed to have been selling moonshine whiskey as high quality bonded goods by using fake labels and counterfeit government revenue stamps, it was learned today.

A raid was made by agents yesterday in which a quantity of fake whiskey labels and counterfeit revenue stamps and two stills were found in a basement of a building in the Italian section. No arrests were made at the time of the raid.

Agents had long been puzzled and had been unable to apprehend the parties who were believed to be selling fake "bonded" whiskey.

When I found this clipping I made copies and filed it away. Its possible significance escaped me for a long time. Months later, when I was reconstructing the various New York stamp cases, the light went on, and I started to put the pieces together. The treasure trove would be a case that would encompass bootlegging, counterfeiting of currency, whiskey labels, revenue, and postage stamps. Then for spice there will be a murder or two.

Another item that began to tie things together was found in a newspaper account reporting the discovery of new counterfeit bills. In a news article found in the *Asbury Park Journal* in December 1922, the director of the Secret Service was lamenting how an increasing quantity of counterfeit U.S. currency was being found in other countries. The article speculated there might be some connection between the appearance of these bogus bills and the bootlegging trade that was sweeping the country.

It is my suspicion that while reports appeared in the newspapers expressing mystification about what was going on, senior law enforcement officials in Washington most certainly knew the source of the bad bills. Unknown to the public, a major undercover investigation had been under way for some time. As an investigation, it was very good. As a judicial exercise that could cut back the sprouting branches of organized crime, it was a complete failure. This is the public record of what occurred.

In Detroit early in 1922, Joseph A. Palma, the local agent in charge of the Special Service Squad of the Internal Revenue Department, received a report of two children who were passing counterfeit notes. (The newspaper reference "Special Service Squad," I suspect, was a reference to the U.S. Secret Service.) Zigmund Rossi, age 14, and Freda Rossi, age 8, had been picked up by juvenile authorities. Their parents, Angelo and Lillian Rossi were brought in for questioning by the local authorities. They did not admit to knowing anything about the origin of the bad bills, or for that matter, that the bills their children had been passing were counterfeit.

Summoned to the police station, Agent Palma questioned her and then examined Mrs. Rossi's fur coat. When he found nine more counterfeit $20 bills sewn into the lining, he knew that her protestations of innocence were false. Confronted with the bogus notes, the story she then came up with was that over a three-year period she had innocently accepted them in payment from a person who had been lodging in her home.

The woman was indignant that her word would be questioned, and decided that she did not want to talk to the agent anymore. In today's legal environment at that point, Agent Palma would have had to stop questioning the woman and let her talk to her attorney. These, however, were pre-Miranda/Escobedo days, and Palma kept hammering away. Mixing truth with falsehood, Mrs. Rossi incriminated herself further.

Palma extracted the story of a lodger who reportedly paid Mrs. Rossi with the bogus bills in return for room and board. She identified this individual as Toto Miliazio and gave the officer a complete and detailed description. Palma carefully recorded everything that was said, and he then went to the Rossi neighborhood to do interviews. It did not take him long to determine that if there was such a lodger, none of the neighbors knew of him. In Palma's view, the lies Mrs. Rossi had been spinning served to prove that she and her family had been knowingly passing counterfeit money on the public. Both she and her husband were destined to become involuntary guests of the government.

Palma's next step was to take the Rossi residence apart. The search did not uncover any more money, but he did find incriminating correspondence that seemed to originate from New York City. The letters he found described various criminal activities, and the agent suspected he was on to something larger than just a few counterfeit bills. Palma gathered up the evidence he had and then caught a train to Washington, D.C.

As far back as the turn of the last century, to keep track of counterfeiting activity, there was a room in D.C. filled with seized correspondence and file drawers overflowing with counterfeit currency that had been captured in previous cases. Many years later this would be the foundation of the Secret Service forensic laboratory. Back then this was a primitive intelligence nerve center.

Besides analyzing the correspondence, counterfeit currency is identified by serial numbers and other characteristics. In this way, the Treasury Department can tell, for example, if counterfeit bills found in California are the product of a new scheme or are bills that could have been missed in some case 10 years before. It also ties bills in one location to other hot spots. It is my suspicion that the department soon determined that the bills in Mrs. Rossi's possession had appeared in circulation in other locations.[21]

Meeting with his superiors in the Treasury Department, Palma laid out what he had found. Then he voiced his suspicion that he had stumbled upon what could be a massive criminal conspiracy. The officials in Washington agreed, and Palma was instructed to open a secret office in New York City. To pursue this investigation he was given the choice of any 30 agents in the United States.

Working with the correspondence from the Rossi residence, Palma soon pinpointed a person he believed was the source of the letters. This suspect also just happened to match the description that

---

21 This is the way it is supposed to work. Sometimes it does and sometimes it does not.

Mrs. Rossi had given of her mysterious lodger. Following this suspect around New York City he was soon observed passing counterfeit bank notes and also selling counterfeit postage stamps, revenue stamps, and whiskey labels. This person was not arrested, but his every move was observed, and each person he contacted was trailed and identified by his Secret Service shadows.

The goal of every counterfeit investigation is to work your way back to the printing press that is producing the bogus items. You can grab street passers (the people spending the bad money) and small-time distributors until you are running in circles, but that does nothing to stop a counterfeiter and his press from churning out more bogus items. To be successful, a counterfeit investigation must work its way back from the street-level passer to the wholesalers, and then eventually to the press. You do this through surveillance, undercover buys, and careful interviews of users and victims. This required much patience, and very judicious arrests. A side note about "victim" interviews. In counterfeit stamp cases, time and again, the agent will find that in speaking to users he will find he has actually been interviewing the printer or members of his immediate family.

To successfully conclude a counterfeit investigation, above all this means time – thousands of investigative man-hours. If the job is done right, and (especially) if luck is on your side, undercover agents can infiltrate right into the actual production and distribution chain of the criminal enterprise. To state the obvious, this does not happen over night, or without danger to the agents involved.

Palma began the job by running down the street passers. He was careful not to make any arrests that would show the government was involved in an investigation. Step by step, the chain of distribution was slowly uncovered and linked together. Months later a major success occurred when Palma was able to insert some of his own agents into the body of the gang.

For some time, Agent Robert L. Godby had been domiciled in New York. On the streets of the city his job was to blend in and masquerade as a criminal. He had been doing this type of undercover work long before he had been reassigned to Palma's task force, and was very good at the role he was playing. People on the street had no inkling that this man who carried a gun and talked tough was in reality a federal agent. He spent his time in the company of criminals and had been accepted as one of their own.[22]

From his inside position, Godby began the delicate task of introducing two other undercover agents to the men he had identified as the suspected counterfeiters. Agent Gabriel Di Fiore (called "Deflore" in some press reports) had come in from Pittsburgh, Pennsylvania, and assumed the name "Salvatore Angelo" (DeAngelo in some news articles). George H. Harris was an agent from Chicago who worked under the name "George Jackson" ("Tom Jackson" in some news reports). The two undercover agents were represented as having strong connections within the banking community and a ready access to cash.

Agent Jackson was a large, muscular fellow who aptly played the role of a thug. Di Fiore aka Angelo, was a mild-mannered, genteel individual of barely medium height and slender frame. He fit his role as a banker, who demonstrated a calm and dignified manner. Both of these men were experts at playing their roles and would never be suspected of being federal lawmen.

With Godby's help, Angelo and Jackson established themselves as pillars of the criminal community, and eventually they met with Enrico Schettino and Salvatore Esposito. These were the suspected heads of the counterfeiting operation. Eventually they worked their way back to a meeting at 365 Broome Street, which was both the center of the counterfeiting plot, and the gang's headquarters.

Greed frequently does overcome suspicion. Days of bickering and bargaining ensued, with Angelo speaking broken English. When he was introduced by Godby, it was as an immigrant of French descent. Godby neglected to mention that in addition to speaking flawless French and English, the agent from Pittsburgh was fluent in Italian as well. Believing they were safe in speaking their native language, those around him chatted away, unaware that everything they said was understood.

The hook the agents used was "Angelo's" banking connections. They presented a proposition to distribute counterfeit money directly into the banking system. If this could be accomplished there would

---

22 This was a program begun by Chief Hazen and then William Flynn. It was the only way they could infiltrate Little Italy in the 1900s.

be little danger to the gang, and they could realize a profit of virtually 100 percent. Godby's underworld acquaintances were interested, but wary. This could be a big operation with a big payoff. The undercover officer suggested that he could take up to $1 million in bogus money.[23]

At one point in the negotiations the criminals demanded to see Angelo's money. This is never a comfortable moment in the life of any undercover agent. A modern-day equivalent to Angelo's situation would be a person being told to show his cash to a guy selling alleged Rolex watches for $100 on a street corner. When the salesman suggests going into a nearby dark alley to complete the transaction, one should get a strong suspicion there may be trouble in store.

The agents didn't blink in the face of this challenge. Angelo and Jackson took the negotiations to a large New York bank. There, under conditions which the agents had under their total control, they displayed their money, and continued the bargaining. This play acting had been anticipated and prepared for by the government. The gang leaders were both impressed, and now convinced of the legitimacy of their new business associates.

At this point the government was trying to buy some time; the agents still did not know where the printing press or presses were located, and they were not ready to move on the gang. The counterfeiters wanted to make a deal immediately, but the Treasury Department was understandably reluctant to let the money they were putting up walk out the door.[24] They had to stall for more time.

Even distant, totally unrelated events worked in the government's favor. In December, the "fake" Angelo had returned to Pittsburgh to spend the holidays with his family. While there, an individual also named Angelo was implicated in a murder that was heavily covered by the local newspapers.

Angelo had bragged that, belying his dapper appearance, he really was a bad man. To buy time he sent his New York contacts

---

23 This is common in counterfeit investigations. Once you have met the distributors you place a large order. You want to get the press rolling again. Another consideration is that the more contraband you can bring into the courtroom, the larger the impact will be on a judge and jury.

24 In the 1970s, Secret Service field agents liked to work with the postal inspectors in joint counterfeiting investigations. Besides more bodies, one big resource the postal inspectors brought to the table was front money. To advance a case, inspectors were not adverse to fronting the "buy money" and letting it walk.

newspaper clippings that described a lurid murder that had been committed in Pittsburgh and for which he claimed the credit. He explained that he would return as soon as he beat the rap. "That Salvatore, he is a good performer," the gang probably said admiringly. They sent word back to him – just give them a date and time, and alibi witnesses would be produced who would swear he had been in New York when the Pittsburgh murder had occurred. If worse came to worse, any witnesses against him could always disappear. After all, what were friends for?

Eventually, Angelo returned to New York with a tale about how he had beaten the case against him. By the standards of criminal society, not only were Angelo and his associates acceptable, they had now established they were men to be respected.

By February 20, 1923, the government was finally ready to make its move. Working from the offices of Captain John F. Tucker, the agent in charge of the New York Secret Service, teams of agents spread out. Before the night was over, at least 20 men and a number of what the press would describe as "stylishly gowned" women, would be in the government's custody.

Tucker's offices soon became crowded as his raiders returned with their prisoners. To maintain the secrecy of what was occurring, Captain Tucker posted guards throughout the building, deliberately cutting off those in custody from any contact with either friends or reporters. While his agents were being debriefed and their prisoners were being questioned, Tucker refused to make any public statements on what had occurred.

These arrests came as a complete surprise to everyone, including the New York Police Department. Fearing leaks of information, the federal agents had systematically excluded the New York police from any knowledge of their investigation. This had been a very deliberate decision on the part of the Secret Service; over the years, more than one sworn officer of the law would be found on the mob's payroll.[25] You can also add to that list a number of judges and politicians.

---

25 One of the darkest days in the history of the Secret Service was when one of its own was arrested in Chicago. He would be charged and convicted of attempting to sell information on an ongoing investigation to a member of Chicago's organized crime. The mobster in question thought he was being set up and filed a complaint with the U.S. attorney. To reiterate, sometimes you just do not know whom you can trust. The agent in question to this day is still protesting his innocence.

The Secret Service probably was correct in its suspicions. In the published accounts, local police officials and political figures were plainly not very happy. They accused the government's agents of deliberately withholding information from them, and generally complained about the way the investigation had been conducted and how they had been excluded. It was only after each prisoner had been thoroughly grilled by the agents that he or she was taken to local police stations for holding. Any of the local police on the mob's payroll were powerless to help those in custody.

It did not take long for members of the press to descend on the customs house to find out what was going on. Reporters were teased with the information that the raids followed the discovery of an organized band of counterfeiters who were acting under the direction of a central group. Only after the prisoners had been processed would stories of the individual arrests be made public.

In the account of one raid in Long Island City, a dozen Secret Service agents descended on a house on Third Street. At pistol point three men and two women were captured by lawmen who swarmed in on them from the roof, windows, and doors. The press was informed that the prisoners captured in Long Island City had been trailed to that location the previous night. A day earlier, these suspects had met with persons who had been identified as the leaders of the counterfeiting gang. The Secret Service agents knew that negotiations to purchase counterfeit money had occurred, and when the counterfeit money was delivered, the federal agents moved in.

A number of New York City addresses had been raided. At 169 Thompson Street several men and women were picked up. Then another squad of agents surrounded a tenement on the Lower East Side. With a signal from a man on the roof, officers crashed through a door that had been reinforced with iron bars. They arrested the occupants at this location and reportedly seized several traveling bags filled with counterfeit money. In coordination with this foray, other federal officers broke into a speakeasy down the street and arrested two men and a woman at that location.

These arrests were dramatic – from both sides a number of gunshots were fired. In the raid that occurred in Brooklyn, one man trying to avoid capture jumped out of a window. Several others fought with their captors and in turn were "roughly handled." When the agents crashed into their target on Conselyea Street, one of the occupants they encountered was their undercover agent, Salvatore Angelo, who was carrying a satchel containing $6,000 in real currency. The newspapers dramatically reported his arrest:

"What are you doing with this?" one agent asked.

"I'm buying some bootleg whiskey with the money," he responded.

"Bootleg twenty dollar bills you mean. You can tell that to the judge," stormed one of the agents as he grabbed Angelo by the collar and dragged him out of the door.

Protecting the identity of their undercover officer, when Jackson started to say more he was hit across the face by an agent, then dragged off with the other prisoners. As the *New York Herald* reported, probably with understatement, "It was a rough night."

Days later, the *Herald* reported, either with a vivid imagination or from inside information, the following reenactment of what happened next:

"Angelo and Jackson were held with the twenty-one other prisoners in the Customs House until morning. 'Stick to your story – booze,' whispered a comrade out of the corner of his mouth. 'We'll stick; booze it is,' said Angelo.

It seems that the gang was not worried by a charge of bootlegging, but counterfeiting – that's a tough one."

All together, in the coordinated raids, 28 men and women had been picked up. One reason Captain Tucker tried to control the flow of information was that he wanted to make sure that all the people targeted were in custody. This was a good decision, and as it turned out the two men they were really after, Enrico Schettino and Salvatore Esposito, had been missed. Before the full story of what had gone on could be released, the government wanted to go after these individuals again.

When information was officially released, the New York newspaper had a field day. Special Agent Joseph Palma appeared before the reporters and conducted a session of show and tell. He began by showing reporters a room filled with counterfeits and some of the equipment that had been used to produce these items. Then Palma gave an edited version of what he described as one of the largest counterfeiting operations in the history of the United States.

Palma presented a bird's eye view of a gigantic scheme to manufacture and distribute counterfeit money, postage stamps, Internal Revenue stamps and liquor labels. He identified the headquarters of the gang as being located in New York City, but he described how the tentacles of this operation spread into every large city in the United States. It even extended into foreign lands.

He told the reporters that before the New York City arrests had even begun, 36 other suspects had been quietly picked up in other cities. Palma speculated that across the country as many as 1,000 persons could be arrested for their role in passing the counterfeits. Demonstrating the size of this scheme, Palma stated that in this criminal enterprise $1 million in counterfeit money and more than $10 million in fraudulent stamps had been distributed by this gang. In its press release the Secret Service never would be accused of using understatement.

Palma described how, more than a year earlier, the Treasury and Internal Revenue Departments had become suspicious of the number of counterfeit bills that were suddenly being discovered all across the country. To combat this, local field offices had been alerted to promptly respond and to follow up on all counterfeit arrests. Banks and other institutions handling large sums of currency had also been told to closely scrutinize all bills, especially $10s and $20s.

Palma stated that, "The similarity of workmanship found in these bills led to the conclusion that they probably came from a single central distribution point." Neglecting to mention his own involvement in identifying New York as the center of operations, he stated that his agents followed the trail, which ultimately had led them back to New York City. Of course, no mention was made of the work of undercover agents.

Fleshing out the tale of the raids, Palma said:

> We set out first to discover the individual passers of the bills. This in turn led to suspects whom we discovered to be retailers, and these retailers

in turn pointed to nine distribution wholesale houses.

So well worked out was the distribution system that we soon discovered one gang of distributors sometimes was not acquainted with another. We tried to get to the wholesalers, but found ourselves blocked by six or seven men guarding the streets in which these operations were going on. As soon as a strange face of an agent appeared everyone laid low and we couldn't get to them.

We often reached the point where we could take ten or more men with the goods on them, but that would simply give the others the cue to skip.

In this news interview Palma was giving the classic bird's-eye view on how counterfeit investigations are conducted and also how counterfeits are distributed. Major counterfeiters generally do not spend their own products – they sell the bogus items to others to distribute and use. Wholesale lots of counterfeits may travel through many hands before they are finally passed on to the public. Be it currency or stamps, at each descending level of distribution, the price the buyer pays increases. An agent can tell just how close he is to a press by the wholesale selling price of the items.

To quote Palma:

An interesting feature of our work was that the closer we got to the center of operations the lower we found the price of the spurious bills. At a considerable distance away we found the bills selling at 50 cents on the dollar. The lowest quotation we got was 17 cents to the dollar. Then we knew we were pretty close to the middle of things.[26]

Palma sounded as if he was surprised by this development, and maybe he was. According to press reports, and the statements from the Secret Service, the 1922-'23 New York case was the largest and most sophisticated counterfeiting operation they had yet uncovered in the United States. It would become a textbook example of agents successfully tracing a counterfeit operation through undercover buys and infiltration. When Palma described the distribution network and the sales structure, he was outlining what every agent is instructed to

---

26 A good way to sort stolen from counterfeit stamps is the selling price on the street. Commonly, counterfeits sell for 50 percent or less of face value. Stolen stamps go for 75-90 percent.

look for in today's training.

The source of the currency and stamps had not been easy to locate. Besides the primary printing plant, the gang also used a number of smaller production facilities in other locations. Complicating the search was the discovery that these printing plants were frequently being moved from one location to another. For distribution just in the New York area, 17 different wholesale houses were identified. When it came time to take these operations down, the agents had their hands full trying to hit all of these locations at the same time.

The newspapers devoted many column inches to pictures of Palma standing in a room filled with the printing equipment and some of the items it produced. The seizure inventory would list all forms of equipment, and most importantly, the plates that had been used to produce many of the bogus items. This inventory included more than $100,000 in finished bank notes, $3 million Internal Revenue stamps, tens of thousands of postage stamps, and millions of whiskey, beer and champagne labels.

Discussing the plates, Palma stated that those items had been made by craftsmen in Italy, and then smuggled into the United States by a simple and expedient method. They had been coated with paraffin and inserted into the middle of cheeses. (This has been a time-honored method of smuggling. Years later it was used by Luciano and Bonanno to smuggle narcotics.)

Spending the bogus bills, Palma explained how the criminals either exploited or enlisted the aid of two different groups. Much of the counterfeit currency was very crude and would be easily identifiable by anyone who examined it. Their answer was simple. Pass the poorly printed bills onto newly arrived immigrants who would be unfamiliar with genuine notes. Another group they victimized were the bootleggers and dope runners. More than one smuggler was reduced to impotent rage upon discovering he had exchanged his cargo for bogus money. What could he do – file a complaint with the police? If he made too much noise, his business associates could easily end the dispute with a bullet in his head. It was this bootlegger connection that gave this case its international flavor. The smugglers transported the funny money around the world, and bogus money from this operation would be identified throughout Europe and the Mideast.

Palma enjoyed regaling the reporters with his tale on how the criminals had operated and the accounts he gave of the government's raids. This story appeared in the February 22 *New York Times* edition:

> We learned recently that the central plant was at 365 Broome Street (the gang's headquarters in lower Manhattan). This was just down the street from the local police headquarters, and there was another plant at 29 Cornelia Street, in Greenwich Village. Then we discovered that a delivery of $10,000 in counterfeit notes was to be made to buyers at a house at 89 Conselyea Street, in Brooklyn.
>
> Benny Sorrentino of that address, we learned, was to be the agent in the delivery of the money, and George Johnson, Salvator San Angelo of Pittsburgh [sic- George Jackson and Salvatore Angelo, the undercover agents]; Michael Trantier, 187 Grand Street, and John Gadena of 161 Grand Street, Manhattan, were to be the buyers.
>
> Our men were at the Conselyea Street house in advance and arrested these five men. We also arrested Salvatore Pottaglino, 18 years old, of 74 Forsyth, who was armed with two pistols, and who accompanied Sorrentino as a guard in making another delivery to Pietro Cauli, who said he lived at the Mills Hotel on Bleeker Street.

On February 21, all the defendants were taken before a U.S. commissioner, and the listing of these defendants might be a handy reference to the sprouting weed of organized crime in the New York area, circa 1923. Twenty-three individuals were charged, and their bonds ranged from $2,500 to $25,000. The only prisoners able to post this bond were the undercover agents, Jackson and Angelo. Attorneys for the other defendants made persistent efforts to have the bail reduced for their clients, but their every such attempt was blocked by Agent Palma.

The government left the deliberate impression that other than the paperwork and the trial, the New York case was now over. It was stated that all the agents would soon return to their normal assignments. In reality, there was unfinished business. The kingpins of the operation, Enrico Schettino and Salvatore Esposito, had been missed in the raids, and Palma still wanted to pull them in.

As soon as Angelo and Jackson had been released on bond, they were sent to Esposito and Schettino to give them a report on what had occurred. It had been learned that they were still holding a large quantity of security paper, which could be used for the production of counterfeit currency. Early in March another raid was staged, and this time these men were arrested. Their bond was set at $3,000 and $10,000 respectively.

On March 7, 1923, the ringleaders were arraigned before U.S. Commissioner Samuel Hitchcock. Both the press and the judge soon noticed two other men standing beside the U.S. Attorney. This was interesting as only two weeks earlier these same men had been standing in court as defendants, and reportedly members of the gang. This resulted in another dramatic news report:

> The Commissioner asked, "Who are these men?" Assistant U.S. Attorney A.I. Menin responded: "If it pleases your honor, they are valued members of the Special Service Squad, Internal Revenue Department. The Secret Service."

The government had invested huge resources in this case. In one capacity or another, more than 130 agents had been involved. Given the effort expended, and the contraband seized, one might reasonably expect major criminal convictions to result. Unfortunately, this did not happen. The penalty for counterfeiting called for sentences of up to 15 years. In New York only three people went to prison, and their sentences ranged from two to three years. Could it be that organized crime and the power and money it controlled was making its presence felt in the U.S. judicial system? That is a rhetorical question.

The only people who would truly experience the government's rage was the Rossi family back in Detroit. The father was sent to the Atlanta Penitentiary for 10 years, and Mrs. Rossi was incarcerated in Massachusetts for five. Their two children were placed in the custody of the juvenile authorities.

The dispositions of the criminal charges in New York were unusual – these defendants were not the type of individuals who you would ordinarily consider likely candidates for rehabilitation. In today's jargon, many of these men were recidivists and would be classed as "heavy hitters." Words like armed robbery, assault and homicide appeared frequently in their biographies. At least two of them even had previous convictions for counterfeiting.

These arrests had not been the result of some harebrained government operation – it had taken a year of very intensive work. The authorities had documented the sale, distribution and use of counterfeit currency (and stamps). Agents had infiltrated the gang and had face-to-face meetings with the criminals, negotiating the purchase of the contraband. It was no accident that when Agent Gabriel DiFiore (Angelo) was picked up he had $6,000 on his person. The Secret Service knew counterfeit currency would be at that location because their agent was there to buy it.

This had been a gigantic criminal conspiracy, and it should be noted they had not confined their activities to the products of the United States. Among the prisoners' effects were found counterfeit Italian lire and Austrian kronen notes. Then the Secret Service also informed the Canadian authorities that Quebec Liquor Commission stamps were also in the items found.

The bogus U.S. currency had been spread across the nation. In some instances entire shipments of tens of thousands of dollars were sent to other cities for distribution. From many locations, groups of men and women swept across the nation leaving a trail of worthless bills in their wake. Regarding the postage stamps, nobody can even begin to guess how many counterfeit stamps were made, distributed and used. The investigation of postal counterfeiting has never been very high on the priority list of the Secret Services.

It is an understatement to say I found it unfortunate that the investigation into the postage aspect of this case was sadly neglected. Time and again the government's agents encountered these items, but it appears that it was totally ignored. Palma justified this by suggesting that perhaps the gang he had in custody had not been the actual printers of the stamps, but then he was looking for currency, not stamps. It is my guess that Palma simply ignored the stamps as being a needless complication. It appears he took the same approach to the homicides associated with these folks.

The February 24, 1923 *New York Herald* reported:

Mr. Palma said that he could find no evidence to indicate that the alleged counterfeiting activities of the persons under arrest have been connected with murder in the Broome Street section in the last few years and that he is making no investigation or reports purporting to show a connection.

Really? At least two homicides are known to have occurred at 365 Broome Street, the gang's headquarters. Had some of the smugglers complained about receiving counterfeit currency as payment for their illegal cargo, and been directed to the complaint department? Palma's conclusion about the homicides is difficult to agree with, but if he was willing to overlook a few deaths, it is not a surprise that some fake stamps merited no attention either.

What stamps were counterfeited in this case? The seizure inventories are frustratingly vague in regard to the postal items, but when Palma described how the counterfeit currency was made, he said that it had been done by the "painted printing process." I am not a printer and my knowledge of the craft is very limited, but this sounds to me like a description of thermography. Then again, counterfeit plates that Palma retrieved from the gang were described as engraved. It is possible they were the source of the Stern stamps, and possibly at least one variety of War Savings Stamps. No final judgment can be made from the information on hand.

One of many difficulties with researching this and the previous 2-cent Washington cases was that subsequent philatelic writers often confuse the stories. It seems that bits of one case get mixed with pieces from another and the story so produced is presented as fact.

Linn's Stamp News of March 21, 1931, contained the following:

If memory serves us right there have been but two instances of actual counterfeiting of U.S. postage stamps. Both attempts have been made with 2c stamps. The first, we believe, was of the 1894 issue with triangles. This counterfeit we believe originated in Chicago. The other counterfeit originated in New York and was of the 2c stamp copies from the 2c offset print.

Mr. C. H. Williams of Green Bay, Wis. has very kindly submitted a copy of this latter item for our examination. This stamp, says Mr. Williams, was received 7 years ago but was just discovered recently. The stamp is on a cover bearing a corner imprint of "Silver Mailing Company, 182 S. 9ᵗʰ St. Brooklyn, N.Y." The cover is addressed to "Fort Howard Stamp Co., Box 380, Green Bay, Wis." It is canceled at Brooklyn, N.Y., June 16, 1924 ...

Was this one of the "Stern counterfeits," or one from West Allenhurst? Could it be a stamp missed in the raids by Agent Palma? Then again, another possibility is that this is yet another printing from a yet unknown source. I wish I could have seen this cover. Being sent from a mailing house does fit in with Edward Stern's original supposition that mailing houses would be good and unsuspecting customers for counterfeits sold as discounted postage in small sheets. Then again, the mailing house just may have been given an offer they could not refuse. It would not be the only time mail houses would be used by organized crime to put their product on the market.

There is another example of a 2-cent counterfeit of this era that was also probably a "Stern stamp." It was offered on April 29, 1989 by Superb Auctions in its sale of the Siskin Gold Medal Collection of Washington-Franklin Postal History. The cover was described as follows: "The Brooklyn Counterfeit, an incredible cover franked with 6 examples, all different plate positions from the offset sheet of 10, in 1923, N.Y. City local usage. The forgers were arrested and prosecuted in 1924. Fewer than 10 covers known. This is the only documented cover with multiple franking."

I am not sure how a cover postmarked in New York City going to Albany would be "local usage." It is also difficult to see why these were called the "Brooklyn" counterfeit (the Stern discovery was in Manhattan; West Allenhurst is in New Jersey; and the Broome Street headquarters of the counterfeiting mob was in Soho, lower Manhattan. There also is a Broome Street in Brooklyn, but it never figured in any news reports of the case. The reference to the offset sheet of 10 could identify these items as being Stern stamps, but if someone was prosecuted for that case in 1924, it is again unknown to me. It cannot be determined from an auction catalog photo if these are of the same printing as the stamps that David Bennett examined in 1978, and which he identified as the Stern discovery. Then again, in 1992, the American Philatelic Expertizing Service certified a block of four 2-cent Washingtons as postal forgeries of U.S. #528, with a note that they were "Brooklyn counterfeits" similar to those on the Superb Auction cover.

In any event, Palma's case was over, and millions of dollars worth of counterfeit money and stamps had successfully been taken off the streets. The Secret Service agents had performed their jobs very ably. If there was a breakdown in justice, it happened in the courts.

It would be a case like this one that, many years later, would eventually lead the chief postal inspector to declare to the director of the Secret Service: "Time out – these cases are important to us. If an investigation is going to involve counterfeit stamps, then the Inspection Service is going to have concurrent jurisdiction." Or words to that effect...

It is my suspicion that this case represented the first time that what we would eventually know as organized crime got seriously involved with counterfeiting stamps. It would not be the last, and all too soon, they would be at it again.

The center for organized crime in the United States was New York City with Chicago coming in a close second. Under Lucky Luciano, some semblance of organizational peace would be imposed under five New York families. The board of directors became identified as "The Commission." Chicago operated independently of New York and worked under the name of "The Outfit" or "The

Syndicate." The tentacles from both New York and Chicago would spread across the country. They all had one thing in common – making money.

THE OUTFIT PLAYS WITH INK
Cleveland – Chicago

One of the most popular story lines in fiction with a philatelic theme revolves around a homicide committed over a stamp. Fortunately for the world of the stamp collector, this is a rare event. The same cannot be said when counterfeiting becomes a part of the equation. This is especially true when organized crime enters the scene.

There is a great deal of confusion (at least on my part) on exactly who produced which stamp in the early 1920s. You have the first two War Savings Stamps described in the April and May 1920 *Postal Bulletin*. Then there was West Allenhurst, the Stern stamps, and what appears to be a well-organized New York mob operation. Finally entering the mix were found some press clippings from Cleveland and then Chicago. Something obviously was going on.

On January 28, 1923, news reports began to circulate that an individual had been picked up in Cleveland when he tried to negotiate $600 in War Savings Stamps. The day before, this individual had cashed $500 in War Savings Stamps, and upon close examination by bank officials, they were identified as bogus. These items were described as being nearly perfect, and a warning notice was immediately sent out across the country.

Things were then quiet until November 16, 1924, when a prominent local attorney was arrested by the Secret Service as he was getting off of a train that had just arrived in Cleveland from Washington. When this occurred, the Secret Service was anything but press shy, and the attorney was identified to the press as the ringleader of a gigantic counterfeiting plot. He was soon joined in custody by four local men who were owners of small businesses. All were of Italian descent.

The authorities charged Attorney J. V. Zottarelli with negotiating $4,200 in bad War Savings Stamps on a local securities dealer. In his defense, the attorney claimed that he had received these items from one of his clients and that he was simply negotiating them as a favor. Of course he had no idea they were counterfeit. With the local businessmen it was a different story. In their case, an individual they refused to identify simply took the face value of the items from their cash drawer, and gave them the stamps in exchange.

With five people in custody, Special Agent William Harper was anything but press shy. He stated this plot had been operating in New York, Chicago, Pittsburgh, St. Louis and many other cities. He identified one New York bank as having negotiated a large number of these stamps. In Pittsburgh, $10,000 worth of bogus stamps had been negotiated, and it was first thought that this was the center of the crime. In that city 14 individuals would be picked up. Then, Harper learned the stamps he had in Cleveland had actually been received from Chicago. The investigation soon shifted to that location.

When it hit the news in Chicago, headlines such as "U.S. stamp plot, and nationwide plot involving millions in Treasury Savings Stamps," appeared. Then, the newspapers mixed in a decidedly gangster flavor with the cast of characters who would be identified. It was a story that begged to be dug into. What was found is a fascinating melodrama.

Discovering the counterfeit War Savings Stamps in a local Chicago bank, the Secret Service had begun the tedious task of tracking them back to their source. Caught in this net was one Ben Newmark, who was a state fire marshal. Besides Newmark, warrants were taken out on other individuals, all of whom were involved in the negotiation of the stamps. Being charged with possessing, passing, and counterfeiting, the local press promptly branded Newmark as the ringleader of the gang.

The public attention this case generated was largely the result of Ben Newmark's involvement. He was a known Chicago commodity as both a politician and as a criminal. Besides the everyday graft that one might expect to encounter, just the year before, Newmark had been jailed for contempt of court in the bribery trial of Governor Len Small. He had been caught red-handed when he attempted to fix the jury.

If Newmark's name had not been enough to grab the public's attention, local events would again put him in the spotlight. On November 11, 1924 Dean O'Banion had been gunned down in his north side flower shop. Witnesses had identified the driver of the getaway car transporting the two gunmen as a woman. While searching for this woman, an anonymous tip came in saying the police could find both her and the shooters in an apartment at 916 Grace Street. When the local police kicked in this door, the person they found was Ben Newmark, in his underwear. Taken to the station for questioning Newmark was less than happy when he was thrown into the holding tank with street level criminals and other riff-raff. He became very unhappy when the Secret Service then arrested him on the warrant charging him with being a counterfeiter.

Leading the federal investigation was an old friend, Captain Thomas I. Porter. He was making his final mark with this case before he retired at the age of 78. He had not lost any of his investigative acumen over the years. Identifying the stamps in Chicago, he quietly began putting together his case. By the end of November he had picked up 20 individuals. Still, he knew this operation went far beyond Ben Newmark and the others he had in custody.

Newmark was actually only a bit player in this melodrama. Some assumptions can be made on how he became involved. As a state fire marshal, Newmark came into contact with Antonio Bambara who operated an eating, and most likely, drinking establishment called the Blue Hours Café. This was the day of Prohibition and it is a fair assumption that Mr. Bambara's Blue Hours was able to stay open because something of value was changing hands between interested parties. In Chicago, if you wanted to get things done, or wanted to keep your business doors open, this was, and in many cases still is, simply the price of doing business. I can only speculate that 1,000 War Savings Stamps (value $5,000) traced to Ben Newmark helped to ensure that a fire inspection did not close Bambara's doors.[27]

Now Newmark was a reasonably bright guy. When he got the stamps, he decided that he did not want to sign and negotiate these items himself because this would have been like giving a guy a

---

27 About every 20 or so years, the Chicago P.D. is rocked with allegations of corruption. One day in the early 70s the Inspection Service took down an entire police district from the watch commander down to the cop on the beat.

personal check in a payoff. Newmark gave the stamps to William Ziege to negotiate, and the following day Ziege signed and negotiated them at the Lake Street Bank. In return, Ziege received $185 and Newmark got the rest.

Working from the bottom up, Porter's first act was to indict Newmark and Ziege, They were charged with four counts of possession and selling counterfeit obligations, and conspiracy to do the same.[28] Then in the November (1924) term of the Chicago Federal Grand Jury for the Northern District of Illinois, Eastern Division, he brought in an indictment for eight more individuals. Moving fast with the information he was developing, Porter then went out and seized a printing plant along with the plates used to produce the counterfeit stamps. At least some of these printing plates were recovered by a diver from the waters of Lake Michigan. This search was being directed from the shore by Olive Meyers, one of the original defendants.

This counterfeiting case normally would have received even greater coverage than it did if not for other local events. Even for Chicago, November of 1924 was a truly exceptional period. This was every newspaper editor's dream/nightmare. Besides the run-of-the mill robberies and hijackings going on, there was a full scale war raging on the city streets between Al Capone and the Irish Mob. With the murder of Dean O'Banion, this battle was on open display.

Whatever assistance Captain Porter might have expected to receive from the postal inspectors was limited. At that time the Inspection Service was completely absorbed in solving, and then prosecuting, the Rondout mail robbers, and they had little if any, interest in stamps. Rondout was the largest robbery in U.S. history, a distinction it would hold until the 1960s. At Rondout, Illinois, a mail train had been stopped, and several million dollars in cash, securities and jewelry were taken. As this is how stamp stock was transported – there may have also been stamps stock.

Besides the money involved, what would make Roundout so all consuming for the Inspection Service was that William Fahy, a "star" postal inspector in Chicago, was accused and subsequently prosecuted

---

28 Did Newmark and Ziege know that the stamps they had been given were counterfeit? One of the required elements of this crime is knowledge. You must knowingly possess, with the intent to use, pass, or sell, in order for the charge to stick. A common refrain heard in interviews with people using the counterfeit stamps is, "I didn't know they were counterfeit–I thought they were stolen."

as being the mastermind behind this crime. Fahy was a maverick investigator who had never played the games. He solved crimes, but was not well loved by his bosses, or for that matter his co-workers. Much of his success as a criminal investigator was based on the close association he maintained with members of the criminal class. When the Rondout gang was picked up, the finger was pointed at Fahy for planning and then setting this robbery up. Convicted of this crime, Fahy would serve the entire 25-year sentence. On his deathbed he was still professing his innocence.[29]

By February of 1925, Porter was ready to go back before the Chicago grand jury. This time he obtained a superseding indictment with 26 counts. The following individuals were charged:

Santo D. Jemalli (Sam)	Jasper Caravino (Guspano Cherevino)
Dominick Sacca (Socca)	Joseph Guerra
Frank Surace (Cicci)	Enrico Bambara (Henry)
Elias Jabour (Eli the Turk)	Olive Meyers
Eli Levy	Charles Leech
Joseph O. Pullia	Antonio Volpe (Mops Volpe)
Sam Borina (Borini – Sam the Barber)	

In his investigation, Porter discovered that this Chicago stamp fraud had been going on a full two years before the government discovered its existence. As the story unfolded, in April of 1922, Santo Jemalli, Dominick Sacca, and Charles Leech met at Verdi's restaurant located at 610 South State Street. Jemalli was the reported brains behind this plot. The conspirators brought in Antonio (Tony) Bambara to finance the purchase of equipment and printing supplies. It is my suspicion that Bambara was also the group's intermediary with local organized crime. The gang would print the stamps. The "outfit" would distribute them.

Their original plan had been to run off the much abused 2-cent postage stamps, and by July 1, they had produced a glass negative, a photo-lithographic zinc printing plate and an unknown number of

---

29 Testifying against Fahy, the individuals who committed the robbery received much reduced sentences. Refusing to admit any guilt, Fahy served seven more years after he could have been released. To the best of my knowledge the only evidence ever presented against him was the testimony of one of the robbers, and the fact that he associated with criminals.

stamps. Still, they were not happy with their first attempts. The 2-cent stamps reportedly did not meet the standards of what they wanted to produce. They kept on working at it. They got new plate-making equipment and by November 30, they had produced 32 photo-litho plates, each containing the image of 400 etched 2-cent postage stamps. They planned for this to be a big operation.

There is no record of how many of these 2-cent stamps may have actually been printed, distributed and subsequently used. Also frustrating was that no description has been found which would give us identification characteristics for these items. One newspaper account stated this 2-cent project was not pursued, but this is unlikely. If you have gone to the effort to produce 32 printing plates, you do not just walk away from it. It is suspected that an unknown number of the postage stamps were produced and put on the market. If the quality of their product matched that of their War Savings Stamps their identification would be difficult indeed. At the very least, this exercise served as a good training tutorial for their next project.

One of these men must have asked the question: If we can make money with 2-cent stamps, why not try an item with a higher value? Recognizing the profit potential that the $5 War Savings Stamps represented, the gang began working on this item. They planned to run off and distribute at least $1 million worth of these items.

Charles Leach was what the press described as the "expert engraver/printer." He had been recruited to actually produce the bogus items. Not being a career criminal, when Leach found himself in the clutches of Captain Porter, he was soon trying to cut a deal. Meanwhile, his co-defendants were doing everything they could to enforce a code of silence. Daniel Perry, a street-level seller, confessed to distributing the counterfeits and made restitution of $35,000 to the government. Suspecting he was talking, two weeks before the trial was scheduled to take place, Perry was shot four times when he walked down the street. The Secret Service picked up word on the street that this was the price he paid for talking.

It is seldom that a criminal case follows the script of a Hollywood melodrama, but this case would exceed all expectations. Antonio Bambara was shot and killed in his Blue Hours Café on South State Street – "knocked off to seal his lips" was the consensus on the street. The government's suspicion was that it had been Bambara who presented the idea of stamp counterfeiting to the "men of respect." With their blessing he had organized the financing for the operation. When things went wrong, and the Secret Service moved in, Bambara paid the mob's price for failure. Not coincidentally, Bambara's death also precluded anyone higher up in the organization than himself from being prosecuted.

The court record would show that Bambara introduced the group to Joseph Guerra and arrangements had been made to use Guerra's property in Benton Harbor, Michigan. This was the site used to print the stamps. To bankroll the project, Bambara went to Mike (Dago Mike) Carrosso, a labor leader of the Street Sweepers Union and known partner of "Big Tim Murphy," both of whom were well-known Chicago criminal and political figures.[30] Also among the other identified conspirators was Antonio (Anthony) Volpe, identified in the papers as a former "confidence man" for Diamond Joe Esposito, the Westside political boss and cabaret owner. In the Capone organization, Volpe had the responsibility for overseeing Capone's various gambling operations. Digging further into the Chicago organized crime files, Volpe was identified as being one of Chicago's most ruthless killers.

When the trial took place with this cast of characters, you had the material for a circus. Scheduled to testify for the government, Charles Leach feared for his life, and was given a full-time Secret Service bodyguard. When the trial began, six additional deputy marshals had to be detailed to maintain order in the courtroom. Even with their presence, glares of hatred and verbal outbursts greeted Leach's testimony, and the judge had difficulty maintaining order. Packing the courtroom with your supporters was a time-honored tradition in "organized crime" cases on both the East Coast and Chicago. Repeatedly the judge banged his gavel and threatened to clear the court. He threatened to send the offenders to jail for contempt.

When the smoke finally cleared, Santo Jemalli was found guilty and sentenced to three years in the federal penitentiary and

---

30 "Big Tim" was doing four years in Leavenworth for his part in the Dearborn mail robbery, sent there courtesy of Inspector Bill Fahy. Tim was looking forward to renewing Fahy's acquaintance in Leavenworth after his conviction in the Rondout robbery trial.

fined $1,000. Dominick Sacca pleaded guilty and was sentenced to one year plus one day in jail. This sentence was vacated and he was re-sentenced to four months in the DeKalb jail where he evidently was not rehabilitated – I found a note dated January 17, 1931, transferring his file to the Department of Immigration for deportation proceedings. Anthony Volpe would receive little more than a hand slap for his part in this case. His sins would catch up with him in 1931 when an immigration warrant was issued to deport him. The warrant identified him as being a lieutenant for Alfonse "Scarface Al" Capone and an associate of Frank Nitti.

The other defendants entered guilty pleas and received sentences ranging from 15 to 60 days to be served in various county jails. Olive Meyers, the only woman in the case, was placed on parole to Captain Porter.[31] Always the gentleman and a person of his word, in return for her help in recovering the printing plates, Porter had come to her defense in court.

Corrupt postal officials did not escape Porter's attention. On January 3, 1925, Albert Eck, a foreman at the Craigin postal branch was arrested and charged for his part in passing counterfeit War Savings Stamps. Under interrogation, Eck confessed to collecting more than $5,000 in commissions for redeeming fake stamps through regular post office channels.

I was disappointed when I examined the criminal court files in the federal archives. In previous Chicago stamp cases, when the document called for a description of the counterfeit item, an actual example had been glued into the indictment. Regrettably in Captain Porter's final hurrah, he did not utilize the example set by Postal Inspector Stuart.

The Chicago records show that Chicago was the source of the stamps found in Cleveland. Thankfully for philatelic researchers, when it came to identifying the War Savings Stamps found in Cleveland and Chicago, we must be forever grateful to Special Agent William G. Harper. He had been very effective in running down first

---

31 In looking into this case, I found an interesting point in Porter's career. In 1901 he had gone undercover to work in a "macaroni" factory identified as the center of a counterfeit dime operation. When raided the ringleader's wife was noticed leaving with a suspicious bulge in her stomach. When checked it was found to be bags of counterfeit coins. The ringleader was an ex-communicated ex-priest labor leader who would go on to be a force in Chicago politics and criminal activity. He was an associate of those who bankrolled the War Savings Stamp case. You just cannot make this stuff up.

the negotiators, then the distributors of the stamps in the Cleveland area. This was not as easy as it sounded. Again victimizing the local immigrant community the common refrain he heard was, "If I talk, I die." Eventually Harper did get to those responsible, and the following correspondence was sent as a memento to Hon. Donald C. Van Buren, the Assistant U.S. Attorney:

Sir:

Joseph V. Zottarelli, Biagio Russo and Nicalo Salupo were arrested on November 15th, 1924 for the violation of sections #151 and #154 of the United States Criminal Code – having in their possession and passing counterfeit $5 United States War Savings Stamps of the series of 1919. These three defendants were indicted on February 20th, 1925, and soon thereafter entered a plea of not guilty in answer to these indictments. On October 7th, 1926 they were all found guilty by a jury and on October 21st, 1926, they were sentenced by Judge Killetts to serve terms of nine, seven and five years, respectively, in the Federal prison at Atlanta, Georgia.

Along with this letter came 12 examples of the War Savings Stamps WS4. They literally defy detection. Not surprisingly, the letter and the stamps ultimately found their way into the hands of a collector. Now if we could only find examples of the 2-cent stamps these individuals had also printed. That would be a discovery. If that is not enough to spur on one's imagination, there was an interesting note also found in early press reports of the Chicago case: "It is believed that the Chicago gang also produced copies of the 1918 War Savings Stamp as well." Anybody ready for a treasure hunt?

7

Some Light Relief and Some Tragic Consequences

Simply because the professional criminal class discovered stamps as a revenue source did not mean private individuals would lose interest in this activity. Time and again, the everyday person would look at a stamp and get his or her own bright idea. Invariably, they would believe that they had an original idea. A good example of this occurred in 1923 at Toledo, Ohio with Anton Victor Winter.

Winter was anything but an innocent businessman. The record would show that he had run "fast and louse" with the law before. Already in the printing business, one day he landed a contract with a local business to produce 40,000 mailing envelopes. A key part of this contract was that he was to supply the envelopes with the postage already affixed. You can guess where things went from there. When the authorities got around to examining the stamps on his envelopes, they discovered they had been made by Mr. Winter, not the Bureau of Engraving and Printing.

Inspiration supported by the profit motive had been a strong spur to action. When Winter seized upon this business opportunity, he went into his print shop and worked straight through for 48 hours. He did not stop until he had produced a printing plate he was happy with. He duplicated a 2-cent Washington A140 based on the 1918-1920 design.

Putting his scheme together, Winter had thought ahead. In the event his stamps would be questioned, he had prepared a fallback plan. At his local post office he purchased legitimate stamps that normally would have met his legitimate needs. This gave him the receipts he could produce to document his purchase of the stamps required for his mailing. He then turned around and either sold the government's stamps on the street or redeemed them at the post office.. You have to give the guy credit. Generally speaking, on its face, this was not a bad plan. Still, it was not bulletproof. If people begin to ask questions and you are the only person in a town using fake stamps, you have some explaining to do.

It was Winter's fallback plan that actually did him in. When he sold his legitimate stamps at his post office or on the street at a discount, this put him in the government's radar. What Winter had not counted on was that fate had taken a hand in his game. A major stamp loss – some $26,000 in stamps – were missing from the Columbus, Mississippi post office. Inspectors throughout the country had been instructed to look for any unusual sales of stamps on the street. When Postal Inspector George Pate began to look in Toledo, the name he came up with was Anton Winter.

On April 19, 1923, Special Agent William Harper went before U.S. Commissioner Frederick W. Gaines of the northern district of Ohio. He requested and received a warrant to arrest A. Victor Winter, charging him with counterfeiting. Specifically, on or about the 30th day of December 1923, he did unlawfully and feloniously make, forge and counterfeit certain obligations of the United States, to wit, two-cent postage stamps. A second count in the complaint was that on the 18th day of April 1923, Winter had in his possession 25 2-cent counterfeit postage stamps.

With the Winter case, it was amazing how rapidly the authorities and the wheels of justice turned. On April 19, 1923, Postal Inspector George Pate and Agent Harper placed Winter under arrest. He was immediately taken before a U.S. magistrate and a bond was set at $5,000. On April 23, this case was taken before a federal grand jury, and Winter was indicted. The next day he pled guilty and on April 30 Federal Judge John M. Killetts sentenced him to two years in prison. In the annals of federal law enforcement, surely few criminal cases have moved as swiftly!

An article in the April 19 issue of the *Toledo Blade* raved about the quality of these stamps: "The product of the plates is the best the inspectors have ever seen. It is absolutely faultless so far as workmanship is concerned, the only defect in the stamp being the inferiority of the paper." After quoting this opinion, Philip H. Ward

Jr., in his *Mekeel's* column of May 12, 1923, gave his own review:

> I have seen a copy on the cover cancelled "Toledo, April 19, 2:30
> P.M." and must say that the inspectors have poor eyes. While the stamp
> is far superior in workmanship to the recently discovered New York
> counterfeit as well as the old Chicago variety it would never confuse a
> philatelist. The work is done by some photographic method and somewhat
> resembles the surface prints. It is the same size as the genuine variety, but
> is perforated 12 instead of 11. The color is correct but the work is heavy,
> none of the lines standing out very well. The paper is somewhat gray and
> looks soiled when attached to a white envelope. It is no doubt the finest
> counterfeit that had yet appeared to defraud the government."

In no time at all Winter would find himself in the Atlanta
Federal Prison. Still, the authorities were not finished dealing with
him. When I located the federal record on this case there was a note
transferring his file to the Department of Immigration. One might
suspect that Mr. Winter soon found himself declared an undesirable
alien traveling on a boat bound for Germany. This suspicion was
confirmed by a 1949 press report of a speech given by Julian T. Baber
of the Secret Service to a Pentagon Philatelic Society in Washington
D.C. Baber was quoted as follows:

> The counterfeiter's operations ended in April 19, 1923, with the
> arrest in Toledo, Ohio, of Anton Victor Winter in whose shop agents
> seized the plates for the stamps and a small quantity of counterfeits. It
> developed that this was not Winter's first clash with the Secret Service, for
> he was apprehended in 1907 in Rochester, N.Y., for making and passing
> counterfeit $2 bills and sentenced in Elmira, N.Y., to seven years in
> Auburn penitentiary. Winter was transferred to the Atlanta penitentiary
> and deported to Germany before expiration of sentence.

Once again Special Agent William G. Harper came to the rescue
of the historical record. In a letter dated October 26, 1927, addressed
to D.C. Van Buren, the assistant U.S. attorney, Harper sent a block of
six of the Toledo 2-cent Washington stamps and a legal-sized window
envelope bearing an uncancelled bogus stamp. The window envelope
bore the corner card of the Johnson Coal Co., Spitzer Building,

Toledo. The letter and the block of six stamps were described in John M. Hotchner's "U.S. Notes" column in *Linn's Stamp News* of November 27, 1995:

> A very nice Toledo cover was offered by Superb Auctions of Torrance, California, in its April 29, 1989, sale of the Siskin collection. This cover is a business-size envelope addressed to Hon. George Effler, Assistant United States Attorney, Toledo, Ohio.

As successful as this investigation had been, the agents still did not get all the counterfeits. The fact that individual stamps were not sold on the open market has made the search difficult. Where a collector may discover one of these treasures would be on mailing envelopes used by Winter's customers. Two customers have been identified: The Johnson Coal Company and the Commercial Envelope and Lithography Company. Working against any additional items being found is the likelihood they were used on mailings and then thrown in the trash, but a few items may still be out there. Look for envelopes postmarked in April 1923 at Toledo, Ohio. If found, such an item would command a very high premium due to its scarcity.

In any study of stamp counterfeiting, one question needs to be asked: Just how common was this crime? My suspicion is that we have just seen the tip of the iceberg. Time and again you can encounter little gems scattered in the general and philatelic press. In my files there is a small clipping, date unknown. The author was Justin L. Backarch. In a few sentences he reported the discovery of a heretofore unknown counterfeit. It showed up in a stamp mixture purchased from a Long Island dealer. It was a copy of Scott #581, the 1-cent Franklin. It is a lithographic copy and appeared to have been postally used. It is slightly smaller in size than the government's issue. It is just one more item to be added to your search list.

A Question of Legality:
A Philatelic Horror Story

Any discussions of the red 2-cent Washingtons can quickly become confusing. Being the common first class letter rate time after time, the 2-cent red/carmine Washington would be issued and reissued. It also became the common target for the counterfeiter. The red 2-cent Washingtons, known as the Fourth Bureau Issue, came out in 1923, and that design stayed in print in a number of forms (perforated, imperforated, sheets, coils, flat and rotary press, and so on) until 1938. It is not always possible to tell which genuine stamp was the basis for which counterfeit version, as the fakers had so many "models" to work from. Then counterfeit copies of this item were so common that sorting out which counterfeit came from which criminal operation is daunting to say the least.

On December 22, 1935, readers of the *New York Times* were greeted with front-page philatelic news "BOGUS STAMP MART REVEALED BY RAID."

Captain William B. Houghton, the agent in charge of the New York office of the Secret Service, made the sensational announcement that his agents had uncovered "a headquarters for counterfeit and stolen stamps." It was right in their own neighborhood, just down the street from the federal offices. Led by Special Agent James F. Carter, Houghton stated that his agents, in a routine investigation, had visited the offices of the National Union Postage Stamp Corporation at 27 Beaver Street.

Jacob B. Hoffman was the owner of this combination stamp firm and photostamp company. He was arrested and held in lieu of a $5,000 bond. In the Secret Service news release, Hoffman was charged not only with possessing 1,000 counterfeit 2-cent postage stamps, but he was also accused of buying "genuine stamps at 80 percent of their value from employees [sic] of Wall Street concerns." Almost as an aside, the *Times* report added that Hoffman was also charged with having sold 100 counterfeit stamps to Herman Herst Jr.

The Secret Service's statements to the reporters left no doubt what the official government view was. "Secret Service agents said that Hoffman, besides selling fake stamps, served in two other capacities –

as a fence for minor employees of financial houses who supplemented their pay by selling their employers stamps, and as a 'retriever' of used stamps which he washed in acid to remove the cancellations. ... Captain Houghton went on saying ... that the National Union Corporation [sic] might be a cover-up for extensive counterfeiting operations." Describing how Hoffman operated, Agent Carter told the *Times* that: "Hoffman would counterfeit a valuable stamp. Then he'd go around to a stamp dealer and, instead of trying to sell it as genuine, would peddle it as a counterfeit. It seems that as a collector's item the stamp had more value than if it were legitimate."

In its fanfare of publicity, about the only thing the Secret Service conceded was that the printing equipment to produce counterfeits was not found in the office. Otherwise, the news releases were designed to leave no doubt in the mind of readers that Hoffman was a major criminal guilty of any number of misdeeds, and he had to be intimately involved in the counterfeiting of stamps. Inflammatory comments from the government's agents would lead one to believe that the man in custody was the reincarnation of Jack the Ripper.

The government went on to describe how both counterfeit and washed revenue stamps destined to defraud the government had been seized in Hoffman's three-room suite. The *Times* said that Carter's men found counterfeit stamps "of a face value estimated at more than $10,000, [and] stock transfer and other document tax stamps worth another $10,000." There were also seven small books containing about 150 $5 revenue stamps said to have been washed of their cancels by being soaked in acetic acid. Agent-in-Charge Houghton then referred to a quantity of $2 revenue stamps that were found; these had no gum. He concluded those items must also be counterfeit. By the time this case would finally go to trial, the number of stamps in question was reduced to 1,000 counterfeit 2-cent stamps and 130 washed revenues. All other criminal charges had mysteriously disappeared.

Working not only with the newspaper files, but also with the court documents, a number of things soon became apparent: first, the raid on Hoffman's office was not the climax of some carefully mounted criminal investigation. At best it was a harebrained operation by an agent without either planning or forethought.

Second, the case agent really had no idea about what he had found. The final consideration was that the Secret Service either did not understand the situation, or the stamp trade for that matter. Eventually they must have realized they were in error. The prosecution became a cover up for investigative incompetence. That is giving both the Secret Service and the U.S. attorney the benefit of the doubt.

Who was this arch criminal, Jacob Hoffman? At the time of his arrest he was about 31; news reports said age 42. Reportedly, he had been an accountant for 14 years before he migrated into the stamp trade. He had been a stamp dealer for some four years. In addition to his buying and selling stamps, he also conducted a small business in manufacturing photostamps. These were perfectly legal, and very popular low-cost novelty items of the time. They were tiny reproductions of larger photographs, gummed and perforated and used much like stickers are today. Think of the photo stamps the Postal Service issues today. To pursue this legitimate business, Hoffman would have had photo-reproduction, perforating, and gum-applying equipment in his office.

Herman Herst Jr. in his memoir *Nassau Street* (7th edition, page 18), had no doubts about Hoffman's supposed criminality (Note: until the 7th edition, this book called Hoffman by the pseudonym "Johnson"):

> Whether Hoffman was operating the photostamp business as a blind for his stamp counterfeiting, or whether he was approached by counterfeiters because of his equipment, may never be known. But it is known that while he was turning out photostamps in the daytime, at nighttime his equipment was turning out pretty red 2c stamps, printing them by a photographic process and perforating them and gumming them with exactly the same equipment that was used on the photostamps.

I submit that much if not all of the above is not "known" at all. As you will see Hoffman was never identified as a counterfeiter except in Herst's writings and the inflammatory comments of the Secret Service that were picked up by the press.

Returning to a profile of Hoffman, he was an inventive individual trying to keep his business afloat in trying economic times. Besides photostamps, he invented a stamp mount he named a "pochette." He then also founded a stamp club – the National Union Stamp Club – whose weekly meetings were well attended by collectors and other dealers for the purpose of buying, selling and trading stamps. Hoffman fell afoul of the authorities when he openly began to sell some counterfeit stamps at these meetings.

Herst reported what occurred this way: One night at a club meeting, Hoffman passed around a sheet of the counterfeit 2-cent stamps. What grabbed everyone's attention was that he pointed out that they were counterfeit, and then offered them for sale at 25 cents a stamp. When challenged on the propriety of doing this, as Herst quoted him in *Nassau Street*, Hoffman supposedly laughed and replied: "They can't touch me! If I sell a 2c stamp for 25c, certainly no one is going to use it for postage and lose 23c. The post office won't lose a penny on what I sell!" From that night forward, Hoffman began to regularly offer the counterfeits for sale to other club members.

Herst himself bought at least one sheet of these stamps. Reportedly this was at the request of Eugene Costales, a well-known dealer. Costales, in turn, gave the sheet to a friend, who in turn passed one of his halves to yet another person. Stamps were passed person to person and at some point came to the attention of the Secret Service. Attempting to find out what was going on, Special Agent James F. Carter had been given the assignment of visiting the local stamp dealers. I have no idea how long Carter had been an agent, but this sounds to me like an assignment that was given to a junior or new agent. Maybe that explains what happened next.

Following the bread crumbs, Carter was eventually led back to Herman Herst. He approached him as a collector, and at some point Herst showed the agent some of the counterfeits. It is unknown exactly what happened next, but it is my suspicion that things went downhill fast. Anyone who has followed Herst's writings over the years knows that he displayed a bone-deep fear/respect for the Secret Service. It is my suspicion that for the rest of his life it was this meeting with Agent Carter that colored his perception of the service.

The way Herst described what went down next was that after he identified Hoffman as the source of the stamps, it was requested that he accompany Carter to Hoffman's office. It is my suspicion that

Herst was not asked; he was told. In return for this cooperation and his ultimate agreement to be a government witness, he would not be prosecuted. Costales, Herst, and Agent Carter all went to Hoffman's shop. Herst would vividly describe his perception of what happened next: "Hoffman, seeing the trio, then raced to the safe and slammed the door shut, and then frantically looked for a place to hide." With Carter brandishing his pistol, the corner was not available, because Herst and Costales already were cowering in it. When Hoffman was led away, Herst went back to work, where his absence had not even been noticed. According to Herst the whole scenario had taken less than 20 minutes.

A much less dramatic rendition of what occurred at Hoffman's office was presented in the *New York Times*. They quoted Captain Houghton as saying that Carter had been out on routine rounds to question stamp dealers. He was seeking information on a reported counterfeit. The National Union Postage Stamp Corporation was on Carter's list. According to the Times, when Hoffman answered the door, Carter simply began to introduce himself and got no further than "I am Mr. Carter, a United States Secret Service agent." Immediately Hoffman "turned a sickly green" and fled to a rear laboratory. Carter followed on his heels and when he saw stamps soaking in a pail of acid, he drew his gun, and called for help. That is a nice, mellow rendition, but unfortunately, less than factual.

Hoffman's business occupied two rooms at 27 Beaver Street. When it was visited by Agent Carter, besides Hoffman, there were two other men and a woman in the offices. When Carter announced his identity and Hoffman fled to the rear room to close his safe, it was at this point controversy entered the picture. When commanded by Carter to open the safe, Hoffman refused and asked to call his attorney. Ignoring this request while he kept the occupants at gunpoint, Carter used the phone himself to call his office and ask for help.

With the arrival of additional agents, intimidation and physical abuse of the occupants reportedly occurred. Every attempt was made by the agents to extract admissions from Hoffman and the other occupants that they were counterfeiters. Finally, after much intimidation, and he claimed physical abuse, Hoffman succumbed to the threats of physical violence and opened the safe. Inside were a few sheets of counterfeits.

When Captain Houghton gave his interview to the press, he portrayed Hoffman as an arch criminal. Great fanfare was made of his dealing in discounted postage and how he purportedly served as a fence for stamps stolen from legitimate businesses in New York. Then he was also accused of operating a loan shark business under the cover of his stamp trading. Houghton stated that the evidence he had was so damaging that it would be turned over to Thomas E. Dewey, the special rackets prosecutor. That is a nice story, but it just did not happen to be true.

There were a number of questions the government never addressed. Was Jacob Hoffman really a counterfeiter, a fence for stolen stamps, a stamp washer, a seller of fraudulent material? Or was he a philatelist, a stamp dealer, with no intentions whatsoever of depriving the post office of revenue? Were any of his activities actually significant crimes? Was there even one actual crime here?

Whatever version of events you wish to choose (and the defense's account at the trial was of interest), the undeniable result was that Hoffman was arrested and charged with possession of the seized counterfeits. For all Houghton's bluster to the press about capturing a fence and a stamp washer, the government did not charge Hoffman with anything related to such activities. If any of Hoffman's activities had been referred to Dewey, most likely he would have booted the agent out the door.[32]

Hoffman was publicly selling counterfeit stamps to other dealers and collectors *as counterfeit stamps.* Possibly he might have been involved in selling previously used revenue stamps that could end up being reused (and helping things along in that direction was a bucket of acetic acid in his office with stamps soaking in it). But in the matter of Hoffman's possession of the counterfeit stamps, there is no indication that he was either engaged in the actual production of these stamps or that he had criminal intent when he offered them for sale. Unfortunately for Hoffman, his arrest and trial were years before the courts would rule that

---

32 When I was a newly minted agent in Texas, I brought a small hashish smuggling case to the U.S. attorney. He took me aside and informed me not to bring another such case to his office unless I needed to transport the evidence to court in a dump truck.

criminal intent was a required element.

The court documentation for this case was found in the New York City Federal Archives. It answered some questions that I had after reading the various published accounts of the case, and it raised new ones as well.

The documents clarified the conflicting reports of the criminal counts on which Hoffman was indicted, listing them as follows:

> 1. He had in his possession washed revenue stamps, namely, 130 stamps of which 125 were of the $5 denomination, four of the said stamps being of the $2 denomination and one of the $10 denominations.
> 2. On December 3, 1935, Jacob Hoffman sold 100 counterfeit 2-cent stamps to Herman Herst Jr.
> 3. On December 3, 1935, Jacob Hoffman had in his possession with the intent to sell 1,000 counterfeit 2-cent stamps. (These most likely were the items that had been found in Hoffman's safe when Carter raided his office.)

In other words, the only criminal charges leveled against Hoffman were that he had in his possession certain contraband items (washed revenue stamps), and that he possessed and sold counterfeit stamps (to collectors, not to defraud the government). No charges of actual washing or counterfeiting were made, which means the authorities had no evidence to offer in support of any such charge. As to possession of washed stamps, one would be hard-pressed to find a beginner's collection that does not have washed postage stamps in it.

With the Hoffman case, philatelic researchers were again aided by the inclusion of actual glued-in examples of the counterfeit stamps in the indictment. In each place where a counterfeit stamp had to be described, examples of the seized items were inserted in the text. A block of eight stamps were used to illustrate count two of the above list of charges; for count three, a strip of six bogus items was inserted.

The trial didn't begin until July 8, 1936, with Judge Vincent L. Leibell presiding. Judge Leibell was a recent appointment to the federal bench by President Franklin D. Roosevelt (one of the most famous stamp collectors in the United States). Although the very first news reports noted the philatelic aspect of this prosecution (one of the *New York Times* headlines was "Held for selling bogus stamps to Philatelist/Alleged counterfeiter and fence seized here by U.S - Collectors prized fakes"), when it came time for the trial no one seemed to know anything about stamp collecting.

Hoffman's attorney left much to be desired. When the jury was picked he managed not to place one person who knew anything about stamp collecting. Not only that, but none of the jury's friends or relatives were collectors, and most of them did not even know this hobby existed. The presiding judge was not much bettor. Hoffman's attorney was described by Herst as being totally ignorant of philatelic matters, and when the trial commenced did not challenge parts of the government's case that would have helped his client. Considering that Herst had already concluded that Hoffman was guilty of dastardly deeds, this speaks volumes in itself.

The first day of the trial was a total disaster for the defense. Besides Herst, many members of Hoffman's National Union Stamp Club were also in attendance and they decided to educate Hoffman's attorney. That night they took the attorney aside and gave him a six-hour course on the ins and outs of stamp collecting. Perhaps primed by his previous night's study, the next morning the defense attorney called Herst, the government's star witness, to the stand.

He first quizzed Herst on a number of items relating to stamp collecting and the stamp business. Then he got into criminal intent. The defense's new approach was to illustrate that Hoffman's possession of some equipment that a counterfeiter might use did not mean that he himself was using the equipment for counterfeiting - his photostamp business required these very same machines. The prosecution was not charging Hoffman with counterfeiting, but they used his possession of such equipment to infer his involvement in this activity.

In the cross examination of Herst, it was established that Hoffman was a legitimate stamp dealer. Then other dealers took the stand and testified about the practice of collecting counterfeits for study and reference purposes. Catalogues from stamp auctions and philatelic publications were introduced as proof of the amount of interest that existed in postal counterfeits and that it was a recognized philatelic specialty. The jury was told that the practice of collecting counterfeits was as old as the hobby itself, and that these items were in high demand.

Hoffman then took the stand to testify in his own defense. He described how he had gotten the counterfeits. His business was buying and selling stamps, and material was brought to him from multiple sources all the time. As he described it, one day he bought a mixture of stamps for $400 from an individual he only knew as Mr. Smalley. It was not until some time later that Hoffman inspected his purchase closely. That was when he realized he had acquired both counterfeit stamps and washed revenue stamps in the mix. The prosecution belittled this story, arguing that Hoffman knew more about the counterfeits than he was telling.

Hoffman's attorney based his defense on the contention that the sole purpose of Section 350 of the U.S. Criminal Code (prohibiting the possession of counterfeit stamps with the intent to use or sell) was to protect the revenue of the U.S. government.[33] He argued that at no time did the prosecution contend, much less demonstrate, that the limited number of counterfeit stamps possessed and sold by Jacob Hoffman were a danger to the revenue of the United States Treasury.

Hoffman admitted that he had possession of a limited number of counterfeit stamps. He also admitted that he had sold some of these stamps at a price that was far in excess of their face (government obligation) value. But he repeatedly and emphatically denied that he had any knowledge about who had actually counterfeited these items, or that he was a part of any criminal conspiracy. His business was buying and selling stamps, and having innocently purchased these items he saw no problem with selling them as collectibles.

In defending himself, Hoffman complained extensively about the treatment that he claimed to have received at the hands of the Secret Service. The following account of Hoffman's arrest is taken from an affidavit that was filed by his attorney:

> I acquired these few stamps in a bulk purchase of thousands of stamps for the sum of $400. When I finally sorted them, I found that the batch contained a few of these washed revenue stamps and a small quantity

---

33 This defense used today would be supported by decisions of the federal courts (see U.S. vs. Cioffi). There is no way that the government's criminal case against Jacob Hoffman would go forward in a modern federal court–if it did, it would be the government's agents who would be facing prosecution.

of counterfeit two-cent postage stamps. I did not, and still do not concede that the possession and sale of these articles purely for philatelic purposes was and is a crime.

At that time, a man now known to me as Mr. Carter, an agent of the Internal Revenue Department burst into my office with one Herman Herst Jr., a dealer and collector of stamps. Agent Carter then asked Mr. Herst if I was the individual who had sold him stamps. When Mr. Herst replied in the affirmative, he immediately left the premises and Agent Carter remained.

Agent Carter then asked me if I had any counterfeit stamps and I made no reply. He thereupon insisted that I allow him to make a search of the premises. I asked him if he had a search warrant and when he replied in the negative, I refused to permit him to make any search.

I then asked permission to contact my attorney but this request was refused. Agent Carter then proceeded to my safe where many of my valuable stamps and collections are kept. This safe was locked. Agent Carter demanded that I open it and I refused. I again repeated my request to communicate with my attorney and attempted to walk into the adjoining room to ask one of my employees to phone my attorney. Thereupon Agent Carter drew his revolver and would not allow me to leave the room and also called to the rest of the occupants and warned any of them against leaving the premises.

He then telephoned to his office and I heard him ask for some agents to come to the premises. About 5 minutes later six or eight agents arrived with guns and blackjacks in their hands. As soon as they came in, Agent Carter said to them pointing to me, "He is the tough guy." Whereupon one of the agents whose name I do not know, struck me several times and kicked me. I was almost blinded by his blows. He then threatened to kill me if I didn't open the safe.

When I still refused to open the safe, Agent Carter again struck me. I saw that it was fruitless to resist any longer. While I desired to open the safe, it took me almost 20 minutes to do so because of the effect of the blinding blows delivered to my face and eye. The safe was opened only because of the beating which I had received and because of the threats of further bodily harm.

When I had opened the safe, they seized almost my entire collection of stamps and other paraphernalia, all of which I claim it was lawful to possess and dispose of, all for philatelic purposes. After making certain seizures from the safe, they called the other occupants into the office and administered a severe beating to all, individually, with the exception of my girl employee, Charlotte Pearl. They tried to force them to admit that they were counterfeiters and they appeared very angry because the answers were truthfully in the negative.

Affidavits were supplied by the other individuals who had been in the room that substantiated Hoffman's story. The agents, of course, denied inflicting any physical abuse on either Hoffman or anyone else who was in his office. The Assistant U.S. Attorney prosecuting the case, John W. Burke Jr., filed an affidavit that denied that any mistreatment had taken place. Speaking from experience, that is what one would expect your prosecuting attorney to do.

Reviewing the court file, I found another motion. It was filed at the commencement of the proceedings and requested the suppression of all of the evidence seized from Hoffman's safe. When Agent Carter entered the office and announced who he was, before Hoffman would answer any questions he asked to speak to his attorney, which was refused. This was 30 years before the courts recognized Miranda/Escobedo (advise of rights and representation by council). He also refused to open his safe (located in a different room) for inspection without a search warrant. This is a privilege that even in the 1930s the court should have recognized.

The jury of non-philatelists was swayed by the defense's arguments, and soon acquitted Hoffman of all charges except that of possession of counterfeits. On July 13, Jacob Hoffman was sentenced to a year and a day in prison, and was fined $250, which Judge Leibeill then suspended. Obviously, the judge had not been impressed with the government's case, or its contention that Hoffman was some dastardly criminal. The judge amended his sentence to one year's probation.

After the trial, the *Western Stamp Collector* commented that when push came to shove, "The Government at no time made any accusation or intimation that Hoffman himself had washed the stamps or prepared the counterfeits, the sole charge being possession." The *Western Stamp Collector* also noted that this was "the first instance when a philatelist has been charged with the crime [of possession of counterfeits with intent to sell them] despite the fact that his sole intentions were purely philatelic, and not a conspiracy to defraud the Government."

It is obvious that I have major problems with what transpired in the Hoffman case. In my view this whole proceeding was a miscarriage of justice. Hoffman may not have gone to prison, but his business as a stamp dealer was destroyed. In the arrest he may or may not have been physically abused, but there definitely was no warrant for the search and seizure of his property, or justification for what the government put him through. Then, he was tried in the press with inflammatory and misleading statements supplied to newspapers by the government. What I found more disturbing is the suspicion that all the time this prosecution was going on, the agents and the prosecutor very possibly already knew or at least should have known where these stamps actually came from.

In retrospect, it can be seen that the conviction of Jacob Hoffman for the "philatelic" possession and sale of counterfeit stamps was a very bad court decision. By this court action, at least in theory, felony criminal sanctions calling for five years of imprisonment and large fines could be extended to serious stamp collectors all over the United States. As Hoffman's attorney told the jury, as quoted in *Western Stamp Collector*, "A verdict of guilty means that over 1,000,000 stamp collectors are today guilty of the same crime should any counterfeit or forged stamp be in their collection." To my knowledge the extension of these counterfeit sanctions to the innocent collector has not been challenged in the courts to this date.

Within the Secret Service, Hoffman's reputation has never been restored – he was "the tough guy" when Agent Carter picked him up in December 1935. He was still a bad guy in the mind of Julian Barber in 1949, when he gave an address to the Pentagon Philatelic Society in Washington, D.C.:

> A few years ago we were called upon to investigate the appearance in New York City of counterfeit 2c postage stamps which were being used in large quantities by unscrupulous business concerns. ... This practice continued for several months until agents raided the shop of a stamp dealer of doubtful reputation and captured a camera and other photographic equipment, as well as gumming and perforating machines, and a quantity of counterfeit stamps.

The impression that is again being left with the audience is that Hoffman was a counterfeiter. Mr. Barber failed to mention what the court had ruled about the "stamp dealer of doubtful reputation" and the outcome of the charges against him.

In 1979, Herman Herst Jr. in his book *The Complete Philatelist* recalled the Hoffman case again. Herst no longer mentioned his own role in the case, but elaborated on the original story as follows, stating as fact what the government didn't even imply in the Hoffman trial:

> Two generations later, in the 1930s, another counterfeit turned up. A firm engaged in the reproduction of photographs which they produced as "photo stamps" found that the returns from their legitimate business did not justify all of their expensive equipment. They decided to produce examples of the current two-cent stamp of 1927 issue (Scott No. 634), and sell them to drug stores, and other business houses which used quantities of them at discount.
>
> One of the officers of the firm was a stamp collector, and he decided one day that while it was one thing to get two cents each for a two-cent stamp, there might be philatelists who would pay more, just to have the novelty.
>
> He brought a quantity of them to a large and prominent New York City club, and he sold a substantial number of them as out and out curiosities. He made it no secret that they were counterfeits. He defended his action by saying, "I do not sell them with the intent to defraud, since no buyer at 25 cents is going to use them for 2-cent postage."

That last is a paraphrase of the quote that Herst attributed to Jacob Hoffman in *Nassau Street*, and the setting of a 1930s photostamp firm in New York City also is identifiably the Hoffman situation, so it is clear that Herst was speaking of this case. But it also clearly goes beyond demonstrable fact, and indeed is not even consistent with Herst's own previous accounts of the same episode.

Herman Herst was one of the most prolific philatelic writers of the 20th century. He condemned Jacob Hoffman as not only a seller of counterfeit stamps, but also as being the counterfeiter. Herst was a respected voice in the stamp world, and it has been through his writing that Hoffman is condemned to this day within the stamp collecting community.

That Hoffman was a counterfeiter was a conclusion that Agent Carter was more than willing to jump to. Surely it did not take the Secret Service long to know they were wrong. Then the prosecution of Jacob Hoffman became an exercise in face saving on the part of the government.

We are still left with the question of where the stamps that Jacob Hoffman had came from. I did find some hints that may just supply the answer. While searching clippings files at the American Philatelic Research Library, I found a two-part article by H. Van Dorn Robinson that appeared in consecutive issues of the *Weekly Philatelic Gossip* (January 1 and 8, 1938) entitled "T-Men Round Up Master Minds of Counterfeit Stamp Racket." The articles are labeled "Reprinted from the *Hartford Courant*." It made fascinating reading.

> While smashing through a secret passageway in an inconspicuous Philadelphia office building a short while ago, Treasury Secret Service men made a sensational discovery – a discovery that was to link Cleveland, Akron, Philadelphia and New York with a nation-wide stamp counterfeiting ring. And which led to its exposure. Cunningly concealed underneath fake drawers and desks was complete equipment for manufacturing and counterfeiting stamps, including engraving plated perforating machines, cameras and gumming apparatus.
>
> Everything was of ultra-modern design and most efficient in operation. Three enormous boxes contained thousands of forged stamps of the current two-cent United States variety, which if genuine, would be worth approximately $14,000.

With possibly some overstatement, the press quoted the Secret Service as proving "conclusively that here was headquarters for one of the largest-scale stamp 'factories' in American history." I've often been amazed at the frequency with which the Secret Service takes down the "largest counterfeit plant in American history."

The description given of the stamps was that they were "close to perfection." Following the leads from Philadelphia to the other cities, certain pawnbrokers came under suspicion. These stamps were found in many locations, but the T-Men suspected the source was actually a New York pawnbroker. They reported that when this individual was picked up he had an engraving plate in his possession, and was responsible for distributing these stamps to pawnbrokers in other cities. When he was arrested, the defense the New York pawnbroker presented was that he was making the stamps to sell to collectors, and not to violate the law. As The *Courant* reported, "The Federal men, of course laughed at the ridiculous idea." I find the similarities to be striking between this pawnbrokers' case and the web that trapped Jacob Hoffman. Could this have been the source of the stamps that caused him so much trouble?

The thing that is most disturbing about the prosecution of Jacob Hoffman is that at the same time his prosecution was going on there were developments in Boston and other locations. This began innocently enough. On June 9, 1936, government agents discovered a stamp racket involving washed revenue stamps. As quoted in the *New York Times* this is what happened:

> Evidence linking several business men in a stamp racket, which is said by government investigators to have cost the government nearly $500,000 in greater Boston alone, will be presented to the Federal grand jury tomorrow. Sales of "washed" $1 to $20 documentary stamps used on deeds and transfers of stocks are alleged.
>
> A Secret Service investigator is said to have revealed that cancellations on thousands of stamps have been erased and the stamps resold for half their original price to persons who have sold them to commercial houses at the full face value. The used stamps were obtained from stamp collectors and other sources.

Ten men, among them Blaine Elmer, the owner and operator of Elmer's Coin and Stamp Exchange, were indicted on charges of defrauding the U.S. Treasury through the use of washed documentary revenue stamps.

Even as this stamp-washing investigation was continuing, a second stamp case in Boston made the news. Reports in the *New York Times* on October 29, 1936, told how an alert postal worker in Boston had "observed a large 'S'" in Washington on a 2-cent stamp. This would be the primary identification characteristic on a printing that would subsequently become known as the "Boston counterfeit."

Subsequent investigation led to the arrest of five men in the Greater Boston area. They were identified as John W. Slayter, age

24; Charles E. Donovan, 36; Charles Quinn, 30; Sam Kaufman, 34; and William Leo Ling, 24. Federal Attorney Francis J. W. Ford told the press that information in his possession "indicated there was a distributing plant in New York capable of turning out millions of the fraudulent stamps. Thousands of the stamps were sold in Boston drug stores." Once again the federal officials hinted at "nationwide ramifications" for this particular fake stamp racket. The five suspects were held on a total of $33,500 bail, and a hearing on charges of counterfeiting was scheduled for November 5.

What's the connection?

In later years, when speaking to groups of stamp collectors, Julian Baber of the Secret Service would tell the story of Blaine Elmer.

> One of the most important cases in recent years was centered in Boston, Mass., following the arrest on May 2, 1936, of a Boston stamp and coin dealer [Elmer] for conspiracy to possess and sell "washed" Internal Revenue documentary stamps. This dealer pleaded guilty October 20, 1936, but before arraignment for sentence he contacted our Boston office through his attorney and told of his purchase, before his arrest, of $500 in counterfeit 2c postage stamps at 30 percent of face from a man who he identified subsequently as William H. Ling, a Canadian.
>
> Agents arrested Ling six days later, when he called on the dealer with 50,000 counterfeit stamps in his possession. Five defendants were involved in this case, but only two were convicted, including Ling, and each was sentenced to one year and a day in a Federal penitentiary. Agents recovered $102,100 in counterfeit stamps from twelve sources. These counterfeits were printed in sheets of 100 from photoengraved plates of good workmanship.

Blaine Elmer evidently decided that it was in his best interest to cooperate with the government, and willingly provided the Secret Service with everything he knew.

Unfortunately, the actual court documents for the Boston investigation could not be located in the federal archives, but the February 6, 1937 Issue of *Linn's* (page 227) reported the following:

Counterfeit Stamp Sellers Jailed

Charles W. Quinn of Roxbury, Mass., and William L. Ling of South Boston were each sentenced to the Federal Penitentiary for a year and a day by Judge McMellan in the United States District Court at Boston after they pled guilty to the sale of several thousand counterfeit 2c stamps.

The stamps in question are counterfeits of the current 2c stamp which first made their appearance last year about April.

In the Boston-area coverage of this case, there was no indication that the press that had produced these counterfeit stamps was ever identified or seized.

The British philatelic authors L.N. and M. Williams published a curious account in the February 1940 issue of the *West-End Philatelist* entitled "U.S. 1923 TWO CENT WASHINGTON FORGERY." No sources were cited by the authors; here is the article in full:

Towards the end of the last decade the owner of a large business house in the United States was going through his accounts.

Things were not as they should be, and one of the main reasons was the enormous annual postage bill. If only that item were not in the accounts the business would show a good profit; but its very existence was dependant upon the size of the outgoing mail – that could not be reduced. In the circumstances neither could it be increased.

Consider the matter as he might, he was always faced with the problem: reduce the postage bill, or be forced out of business; reduce the amount of mail, and increase the loss, with the inevitable result. His astute mind saw only one way out of the impasse. The postage bill must be reduced and the amount of mail kept constant.

Although certain stamps could be bought privately at a discount off face value, the supply was insufficient to meet his requirements and the discount would scarcely repay the inconvenience of collection. The only feasible answer was to make his own stamps and print as many as he needed. He was untroubled by any scruples as to the morality of the idea, and he had in the past sailed near enough to the wind not to be worried unduly by the possibility of legal consequences.

Among his acquaintances were numbered two men, bookbinders and printers, who were not above the counterfeiting of treasury bills, naturalization certificates and other public documents, and who each served a term of imprisonment for these activities.

The workmanship of these two men attained to a high degree of skill. However, in approaching them the business man made his first slip, for, deplorable as it may be ethically, it is a fact that the police take an interest in the subsequent doings of those who have been in conflict with the law. Actually, the two men were under surveillance when he approached them.

They agreed to prepare a plate and print forgeries of the current 2 cent stamps bearing the head of George Washington, that being the denomination he used most frequently...The craftsmen set to work. They took as their model a single, clearly printed specimen of the 2-cents stamp. They copied it and built up a plate capable of printing sheets of 100 impressions. Trial printings were made; the sheets were gummed and perforated. The businessman expressed his satisfaction at the result, and ordered a larger printing.

Before it could be made the printers' premises were raided by United States Secret Service agents and Post Office inspectors. The two men were arrested and the printing plant and the plate were seized, together with many sheets of gummed paper and a quantity of ink, besides all stamps found on the premises.

All this happened nearly ten years ago. A considerable number of the sheets which formed the trial printings eventually passed into the hands of some stamp dealers. In addition, a parcel of the stamps was hidden by the two men.

Towards the end of 1935 Jacob B. Hoffman, of the National Union Postage stamp Corporation in New York, sold a sheet of the forged stamps to a well-known member of a prominent stamp club in Bronx. [here follows an account of the Hoffman case, as quoted in the New York Times]

The parcel of forgeries hidden by the two printers before they were arrested ten years ago came to light in October 1936. The stamps had been sold to drug stores in Boston, Mass., and thus came into circulation. They were used on correspondence and noticed by a postal clerk.

The tale of the cost-cutting businessman is realistic – it has happened before in the annals of contraband postage – and leads smoothly into the description of the Hoffman arrest and trial and then into a description of the counterfeits themselves. The story also accounts neatly for the existence of the counterfeit stamps in both New York and Boston. But was this article fact, fiction, or a mixture of the two? Years ago I contacted one of the authors and inquired into their source. All he could tell me was that the person who gave them the details had been a government agent.

The point that really bothers me is that if, years earlier, the counterfeiters had been arrested, the Secret Service and the U.S. attorney should have known this. They would have been ethically bound to make that fact known to the court when they prosecuted Jacob Hoffman in 1936. Today, this kind of evidence is called Brady material, and failure to disclose such information would be automatic grounds for dismissal.

I have not been able to locate any verifiable evidence of the origins of the 1935 New York–Boston 2-cent Washington counterfeit. From the perpetrators' viewpoint, this would be a successful criminal endeavor whose origins at least from the general public remained concealed. For an unknown period of time, these bogus stamps were available, and being used without detection in the mail. In discussing the counterfeits in his column in *Stamps* on February 1, 1936, George Sloane went on at some length about the quality of these items. This is in contrast to a disparaging appraisal by a Bureau of Engraving official.

> John C. Rout, Supt. of Siderographers of the Bureau of Engraving and Printing, recently addressed a gathering of collectors at a meeting of the Washington Philatelic Society, and it is reported, discussed the New York 2c counterfeit and exhibited specimens. He found that the workmanship was very poor and "produced little but laughter from those who were familiar with the Bureau's product." Government scientific instruments showed the faked stamps to be one-thousandth of an inch thinner than the Bureau's specifications demand, and enlarged photographs of the stamps proved them to be short in size from top to bottom, and from left to right ...
>
> While I dislike to disagree with any of the Bureau's experts, I felt, and so did the Secret Service men who saw these stamps, that it was an excellent counterfeit and extremely dangerous. Of course there were minor imperfections in the design – it was a counterfeit – but nevertheless they were circulating freely, and, so far as the government experts were concerned, they probably would be going yet, if it were not for the fact that their distribution was rudely interrupted ... I'd like to bet Mr. Rout one of my Farley imperfs against one of the counterfeits, that he couldn't pull the

fake out of a derby hat if it was tossed in with a mixture of the common, ordinary, every day two-centers.

It is evident that this particular counterfeit stamp was widely distributed, and to this day it is frequently encountered in collector circles and occasionally in the marketplace. Some philatelic articles have confused this stamp with the counterfeit identified by Edward Stern in New York City in January 1922. Even a cursory comparison of examples of the Stern and the Boston stamps should dispel that idea.

The fakes were described in January 1936 by George Sloane as follows:

> The counterfeit was printed in sheets of 100, with full margins but no plate numbers ... obviously made in imitation of the rotary press stamps in that the spacing of the various subjects was the same. Under close examination they resemble stamps printed by the offset process although they were most likely produced from an electrotyped plate, probably of zinc. The carmine color was well matched and in general appearance the stamp was a counterpart of the original, except that it was a small fraction shorter in height and in width. Those I have seen are perforated 11.5, and while on some the gumming and perforating was crudely done, on others the product was as fine as the Bureau produces daily.

This fake has been found in both single and block format; an unknown number of covers bearing the counterfeit also exist. Jacob Hoffman may not have been costing the Post Office Department revenue, but someone sure was. Two different perforating machines are known to have been used: One of 11.5mm, the other produced a ragged sewing machine perforation. The most distinct feature of this stamp is the enlarged "S" in Washington.

Another Twist to the Story
Dateline: Akron, Ohio, May 2, 1936

Stanley A. Mack, a young "stamp enthusiast" pursuing his interest by checking rubbish heaps, found an envelope with what he thought was an unusual 2-cent stamp. Mack took his find to Stamp Dealer Walter T. Popenger, who measured it and discovered it was perf 12 rather than 11, as it should have been. Popenger took the stamp to the local postmaster, R.C. Witwer, who immediately called in the postal inspectors. The mailing envelope was traced to an automobile company in the area where 49 more such stamps were recovered. A mechanic at the business had obtained the stamps from a relative.

The mechanic's relative was arrested and more of the stamps, $28 face value, were found in his possession. The suspect claimed to have received them in lieu of cash for merchandise he had sold to a Cleveland pawnbroker. After checking the story, agents released the suspect but "declared themselves interested in locating the source of the stamps, believed to be in a large eastern city."

On November 25, 1936, *Western Stamp Collector* reported that the then current counterfeit 2-cent stamps appeared in Chicago, "these past three weeks," part of a group of 500 sent to Numismatic Book Publisher Charles Green in the city as payment for coin books ordered by a "Boston, Mass, stamp dealer" (surely Blaine Elmer, proprietor of Elmer's Coin and Stamp Exchange). About 270 of the bogus stamps were used for postage before the Boston source informed Green the stamps were bad and should be returned to Boston for the federal authorities. The article doesn't confirm that Green obeyed the request, but does state that he quickly checked his wastebasket and retrieved several of the fakes. One strip of three was on an airmail cover postmarked Swansea, Mass.

TECHNICAL DETAILS OF THE 1935 NEW YORK/ BOSTON COUNTERFEIT

Probable stamp being counterfeited: U.S. Scott #634

This is an excellent counterfeit of relatively high-quality plate work and printing. The most pronounced identification points are the misshapen "S" and "H" in "WASHINGTON." The S is enlarged relative to the other letters, and the H is "crossed obliquely," as H.G. Leslie Fletcher called it in *Postal Forgeries of the World* (Fletcher's illustrations are good, but surprisingly he mentions only the H flaw, and not the S, which is the more readily identifiable trait). These flaws recur from one stamp to another, indicating that the step-repeat printing process was used to produce the printing plate – one item is photographed, the negative touched up and then this image is duplicated over and over to produce the master printing plate. An error on the original stamp impression will be common to all the stamps produced by that printing plate.

The paper and the gum on the counterfeit are good imitations of the original, and the ink shade is an excellent match. This counterfeit most likely was produced by offset lithography printing. As far as perforations, another of the traits of this counterfeit is what Martin Armstrong called the "sewing machine" perforations: the stamps look like a blunt needle had punched somewhat at random so the resulting torn edge is very ragged.

But the counterfeit also is found with ordinary perfs of gauge 12 and 14. I have two stamps that came off the same plate, and one is perf 12 and the other is 14. Access to more than one perforator would be an indication of a very sizable and most likely professional printing operation. One perforator is hard enough to find, let alone a second one. Throw in the "sewing machine" perforation, and we are looking at three machines at least.

To further complicate matters, I have another #634 2-cent Washington, also perf 12, but the printing quality does not match that of the other stamp, nor did it come from the plate that produced the Hoffman stamps. This stamp has a dirty, blotchy appearance; I suspect that it might be one of the stamps described by *Linn's* in January 1933: "Crudely printed counterfeits of the 2-cent present Washington issue... Any philatelist should be able to tell these counterfeits instantly." Is this a "new, unidentified counterfeit"?

What do I suspect happened with the Jacob Hoffman case??

The simple answer is that this is a bad movie I have seen before. When Agent Carter walked into Hoffman's office he had no idea what he had found or the slightest idea how the stamp business operated. As a federal agent who investigated counterfeit currency, he had a preconceived belief that Hoffman was involved in counterfeiting. Not uncommon in law enforcement, he looked at everything in terms of black and white.

Even after it was evident that Hoffman was not a counterfeiter, Carter's supervisor backed up his agent. When he went public with his interviews, everyone became cemented into their positions. Now the government could not back down and admit it was mistaken. The result was a trial that should not have taken place. The end result was that bad case law was established and technically is still with us to this day.

8

Odds and Ends

Is it Illegal to Collect Counterfeit Stamps?

Virtually since the day the first counterfeit stamp was found in the United States, the argument has raged in the philatelic community about whether these items should or could legally be collected. To virtually all serious collectors, a bogus item is a treasure to be acquired and promptly squired away. It is a collectible, and also a research and reference tool. With the Secret Service there never has been any confusion or question: These items are contraband; they are illegal; we want them; and we want them now.

From the government's point of view, United States postage stamps are exactly the same as United States currency. By federal statute (18 USC, Section 8) and by court decision, both money and stamps are obligations of the government. Any counterfeit examples of either are subject to seizure by the government. Furthermore, while enforcing this prohibition, a collector of counterfeit stamps was threatened with criminal prosecution (Hoffman).

While laws may stand, attitudes change. What was considered illegal in the past may not be judged so today. Our law books are replete with statutes which are no longer enforced. In the official mindset of the 1930s there was no doubt. Possession of counterfeits was against the law. The federal government had the right to seize them, and quite possibly you could be prosecuted. In today's world, if push came to shove, it is questionable if the courts would still maintain that interpretation.

When one looks at United States law, it is important to remember that our legal concepts are not written in stone. Law in the United States is commonly a moving target as statutes are subject to review and reinterpretation. Then also it is not uncommon to find a difference between what may be the letter and what may be the spirit of a given law.

In examining the question of legality, the logical first step is to actually look at the counterfeiting statutes. This topic is addressed frequently. On these occasions I have been amazed at how often it is evident the writer has not checked to see what the statutes actually say. The following counterfeiting laws are currently on the books in the United States.

The federal law that prohibits counterfeiting:

18 USC 471: Whoever, with intent to defraud, falsely makes, forges, counterfeits, or alters any obligation or other security of the United States, shall be fined no more that $5,000 or imprisoned not more that fifteen years or both.

This statute covers not only currency but stamps as well. In the United States, the post office was established by our constitution. The revenues it generated went into the general treasury. By both federal statute (18 USC section 8) and by court decision, both U.S. currency and stamps are recognized as obligations of the government. With the continuing evolution of the post office into an independent agency, some day this will raise an interesting legal question of just how long postage stamps will be considered obligations of the government.

An interesting philatelic case under this statue is U.S. v. Errington. In this prosecution Errington purchased a sheet of 16-cent air mail special delivery stamps and then treated it with a dye to simulate a color error. Errington was convicted of counterfeiting in that with the intent to defraud he altered an obligation of the United States.

The law that prohibits the placing of counterfeit obligations in circulation:

(Possession or selling of counterfeits)

18 USC 472: Whoever, with intent to defraud, passes, utters, publishes, or sells. Or attempts to pass, utter, publish or sell. Or with like intent brings into the United States or keeps in possession or conceals any falsely made, forged, counterfeited, or altered obligation or other security of the United States, shall be fined not more than $5,000 or imprisoned not more than fifteen years or both.

The key word here is intent. This is a basic element of the crime. If the government cannot establish that there is a criminal intent to defraud, there is no criminal violation. In any criminal violation, you must establish that each of the elements of a crime has been meet. This statute covers possession of counterfeits, but for this possession to be a criminal violation there must be criminal intent.

The law that prohibits dealing in counterfeits:

18 USC 473: Whoever buys, sells, exchanges, transfers, receives or delivers any false, forged, counterfeited, or altered obligation or other security of the United States, with the intent that the same be passed, published or used as true and genuine, shall be fined not more than $5,000 or imprisoned not more than ten years or both.

The intent must be that the item being sold or transferred will be utilized as would the genuine article. If you make a sheet of counterfeits that you intend to utilize as a table cloth, this is not a violation of this statute (U.S. v Cioffi). The bogus item must be able to pass as a representative copy of a legitimate item, and the intent to defraud the government in this use must be established. This statute does not cover possession.

There are other Treasury statutes that can deal with counterfeiting. Sections 474, 476 and 477 of Title 18 United States Code deal with counterfeiting tools and plates. Sections 478, 479, 480 and 481 deal with counterfeiting of foreign obligations and securities. The terminology in these statutes is basically the same as found in the preceding examples. To supplement the Treasury laws, postal statutes have been passed which are specifically aimed at protecting the revenue of the postal establishment. It is common for both the Treasury and the Postal statutes to be used together.

Postage stamps, meters and postal cards:

18 USC 501: Whoever forges or counterfeits any postage stamp, postage meter stamp, or any stamp printed upon any stamped envelope or postal card, or any die, plate, or engraving thereof: or whoever makes or prints, or knowingly uses or sells, or possesses with intent to use or sell, any such forged or counterfeited postage stamp, postage meter stamp, stamped envelope, postal card, or die, plate or engraving: or whoever makes or

knowingly uses or sells, or possesses with intent to use or sell, any paper bearing the watermark or any stamped envelope, or postal card, or any fraudulent imitation thereof; or whoever makes or prints, or authorizes to be made or printed, any postage stamp, postage meter stamp, stamped envelope, or postal card, of the kind authorized and provided by the Post Office Department or by the Postal Service without the special authority and direction of the department or Postal Service; or whoever after such postage stamp, postage meter stamp, stamped envelope or postal card has been printed, with the intent to defraud, delivers the same to any person not authorized by an instrument in writing, duly executed under the hand of the Postmaster General and seal of the Post Office Department or the Postal Service, to receive it – shall be fined not more that $500 or imprisoned not more than five years or both.

USC 501 does cover possession, but again there must be established that this possession was with the intent to use or sell. Use has been defined as postal use. If there is no criminal intent to use these items in the mail, and thus deprives the Postal Service of revenue there is no violation of this statute. In the late 1990s there was an incident in Chicago where two artists produced facsimiles of stamps as artworks. Any prosecution under this statute would be rejected not on the use argument, but two other grounds: First, the items are not copies of existing stamps and should not be confused with legitimate stamps, and secondly, it can be argued that the intent was not criminal.

The doctrine of postal **"use"** is supported by the congressional intent that is found in the original postal counterfeiting statute:

> 5 Stat 749 (1845) ... If any person shall forge or counterfeit, or shall utter or use knowingly, any counterfeit stamp of the Post Office Department or the United States or the Post Office stamp of any foreign government, he shall be adjudged guilty of (a) felony ...

In this initial statute, there is no provision that would prohibit the sale of counterfeit postage stamps. Subsequent judgments and court interpretations of this statute have taken it to mean that, by specifically condemning "use" of counterfeit stamps, the purpose of Congress in enacting this law was to protect the revenue of the post office.

In the postal statutes, postage and revenue stamps of foreign governments are specifically covered under 18 USC 502. This statute covers counterfeiting, uttering, and using; it does not address the topic of possession.

A major development in the interpretation of the counterfeiting laws occurred with the prosecution of United States v. Cioffi. This individual was arrested after the sale of counterfeit 8-cent Eisenhower stamps to an undercover Secret Service agent. He was convicted of violating 472 (makes, forges, counterfeits). The Court of Appeals in reversing this conviction made the distinction that simple possession was not enough to determine guilt: There must be intent to commit a criminal act. Cioffi was promptly then charged and convicted of violating 501 – possession with intent to use, or cause to be used in the mail.

The common element of intent is necessary to sustain a criminal conviction in each of the counterfeiting statutes. The authorities must establish, beyond a reasonable doubt, that the defendant intended to commit a specific criminal act. Under each of the counterfeiting statutes, to simply possess counterfeit postage, absent criminal intent, is not a crime. Unfortunately, for Jacob Hoffman, who was a New York stamp dealer who sold counterfeit stamps as identified counterfeits to collectors, this legal interpretation came too late.

Bogus postal items have both a strong and abiding collector interest and value. For collectors they are possessed with no intent whatsoever to defraud the government. The simple possession of a counterfeit stamp does not by itself constitute a threat to the revenue of the Postal Service. They are legitimately collected and researched, and all over the world that has been so since the day stamps were first issued.

With present-day legal interpretations, if a collector was confronted for simple possession of a counterfeit stamp, I doubt if he could be legally prosecuted. In today's world, if the Hoffman case was presented to a U.S. attorney, the agent would be laughed out of the office. Possession is used as a hammer to seize items and get as much of the product as possible off of the street. This raises the question – can bogus postal items be legally seized from collectors by government agents? The blanket right to seize is based on the supposition that the mere possession of these items is a violation of Section 492 of the United States Code, "Forfeiture of Counterfeit Paraphernalia."

All counterfeits of any coin or obligation or other securities of the United States or of any foreign government, or any article, device, or other things made, possessed, or used in violation of this chapter, or of sections 331-333, 335, 336. 642, or 1720 or of this title, or any material or apparatus used or fitted or intended to be used, in the making of such counterfeits, articles, devices or things, found in the possession of any person without authority from the Secretary of the Treasury or other proper officer, shall be forfeited to the United States.

The sections referred to above are as follows:
Section

331	Mutilation and falsification of Coin
332	Debasement of Coins, Alteration of scales
333	Mutilation of National Bank Obligations
335	Obligation of Expired Corporations
336	Circulation Obligations
642	Tools and Material for Counterfeiting
1720	Cancelled stamps and Envelopes (washed stamps)

My legal reasoning may be faulty. I am not an attorney; however, if 492 is the justification for seizure from collectors, I see a problem. In the wording of the statute, to be forfeit, the counterfeit must be "possessed in violation of this Chapter." If I am correct that simple possession, absent criminal intent, is not a violation of the underlying criminal statutes (472, 473, 501, or 502), then by extension there is no "legal" foundation for forfeiture for simple possession. Forfeiture can possibly still be justified on the grounds that the bogus postal item is "a counterfeit obligation," but that is a legal position that I also suspect is very much open to question.

Under Title 18 USC 501, "Use" is defined as postal use. To sustain a conviction, you must show that the intent was to deprive the post office of revenue; therefore, absent the intent of defrauding the post office, there is no violation of this law. This position is supported when one sees the manifest Congressional purpose in establishing the original postal counterfeiting statute, cited here:

> 5 Stat 749 (1845)....If any person or persons shall forge or
> counterfeit, or shall utter or use knowingly, any counterfeit stamp of the
> Post Office Department of the United States, or the Post Office stamp of
> any foreign government, he shall be adjudged guilty of (a) felony ...

In this initial statute, there is no provision that would prohibit
the sale of counterfeit postage stamps. Subsequent judgments and
court interpretations of what has become known as 501 have taken it
to mean that, by specifically condemning "use" of counterfeit stamps,
the purpose of Congress in enacting this law was to protect the
revenue of the post office. Judge Fred Friendly wrote the following:

> Both the context and the history of the statute indicate that "use"
> in 501 means use for a postal purpose, not "use" in a broader, colloquial
> sense. It is hard to believe, for example, that the knowing use of bogus
> stamps for a table-cover or wall decoration would violate 501.
> U.S. v. Cioffi, 2nd Circuit Court of Appeals June 21, 1973

It can be argued that there is no legal justification for the
possession of counterfeit currency – bogus currency always being
an immediate threat to the revenue of the Treasury, and subject to
seizure.[34] This is a difficult argument to extend to the possession of
counterfeit postage stamps in the hands of legitimate collectors and
or reference libraries. Counterfeit postage has a value as a collectible
item that is far in excess of its face value. The U.S. Treasury is
not threatened by a collectible fake that no rational person would
squander for use on ordinary mail, for the purpose of having that item
delivered. Then again put that bogus stamp on an envelope, mail it to
yourself, and you have just created a philatelic treasure.

At the time of his trial, Jacob Hoffman made this argument, and
lost. Would he have been wise to appeal the judgment of the lower
court in 1936? Impossible to say, but in 1973, the same grounds that
were used for Hoffman's defense were argued before the Court of
Appeals, and this time the federal court found this acceptable. In the

---

34 I have recently discovered that counterfeit currency is also a collectible commodity. This is mostly
old discontinued bank notes, but I can only guess at the interest to a collector if one could find the
English 5pd bank note. This item was masterfully copied first by the Germans and then years later by
an English master counterfeiter. The latter was tripped up by an American stamp collector who while
riding with a London cab driver expressed his interest in counterfeit stamps.

1973 Cioffi decision, Judge Friendly cited the same argument that Hoffman did: "If you do not have criminal intent to defraud, then the government does not have a violation of law."

Let me throw another wild card in here. In the 1970s the U.S. Post Office became the United States Postal Service – a government corporation. As such the Postal Service is no longer expected to be dependent on the Treasury. It hasn't quite worked out that way, but it does raise the legal question – should stamps still be considered an obligation of the Treasury? Just a thought to further muddy the water.

There was a time when the public as a whole would blindly obey the dictates of the government and its agents. Those days are no more. In law enforcement and judicial circles there is a saying to the effect that excessive enforcement leads to bad or restrictive court rulings. The prosecution or seizure of counterfeits held for collection, study, or reference is a case of excessive enforcement just waiting to happen.

The sand is already washing away from the legal foundation that would support stamp seizure. The following was cited in a column by Canadian stamp columnist Kenneth W. Pugh in *Linn's Stamp News* of October 13, 1975, regarding the seizure of collector-held counterfeit stamps of "dead Countries":

> ... on April 26, 1974, acting upon a "Notice of Motion for the Return of Property Unlawfully Seized," filed by attorney George P. Coulter, March 15, 1974, in United States District of California, Chief Judge Edward J. Schwartz ruled that Ryukyu Mozo facsimile sheets be returned when the U.S. Attorney responded to the motion with the following reply: "Notice is Hereby Given by Respondent, United States of America, that it does not Oppose Petitioner's Motion for Return of Property Seized by Agents of the Secret Service."

Some day, probably with the best of intentions, a federal agent will go too far and counterfeit stamps that are part of someone's collection will be seized. If this becomes a *cause celebre*, and the courts perceive an enforcement excess, future investigative restrictions will be imposed on the government's agents. This would not be in the best interest of either the Treasury Department or the public it serves. For revenue protection it does not help when some mindless bureaucrat or law enforcement agent deliberately antagonizes the first and probably best line of defense, the stamp collector. Of course, even when "helping" the authorities, the stamp community has its own way of manipulating events. In reporting on the Jacob Hoffman case, *Linn's* shared the following anecdote (February 1, 1936:297):

2c counterfeit

A new counterfeit 2c U.S. was turned up in a raid in New York recently and of course the government confiscated all copies on hand. Many years ago a dealer told the writer of helping the officials run down another counterfeit, and he went on, "And, you know, those fellows then took away every copy I had. Wouldn't even let me keep one for my own collection. At least, they thought they did," he drawled.

One must wonder how many times, after discovering some new counterfeit, a collector has refrained from contacting the authorities because he did not want to lose his newfound treasure. I know for a fact that this has happened. Since at least 1900 the United States Treasury Department has been very outspoken on the right of its agents to seize counterfeits. There has been a noticeable silence on this topic since the mid 1970s. At some point in time, collector counterfeits will be seized again. Challenged in court, this time around the odds are that the government just may lose.

A wild card in this equation is the tens of thousands of rules and regulations that have been pushed through Congress in recent years. This is especially relevant with seizure rules implemented to combat the widespread counterfeit merchandise problem. I am sure that somewhere in the reams of documents some budding agent can find some justification to kick in some collector's door.

With the Postal establishment, its revenue has been under continual attack since at least 1894. The public does not have the expectation that such ordinary items like a stamp would be counterfeited. If in recent years counterfeit activity has diminished it is because general utilization of the mail by the public has been curtailed. We now have other ways to communicate rather than putting a stamp on an envelope.

For the Stamp Collector
A Definition of Terms

Some comments are required, and terminology needs to be clarified about the different forms of stamp fraud. The world of bogus stamps is an extensive one that encompasses a multitude of sins. When one begins to explore this world the first problem you face is defining your terms. The words counterfeit, fake, and forgery should not be considered as being interchangeable and careful speakers and readers acknowledge the differences. Here are the definitions that I use:

A counterfeit stamp is a fraudulent imitation of a genuine stamp. It has been produced with the specific intent of passing it off as a genuine article. Simply put, counterfeit stamps are "totally bad," beginning with the paper they're printed on, up to and including all other elements of the finished product. Counterfeits fall into two categories: either postal counterfeits, designed to defraud the postal authorities, or philatelic counterfeits, intended to defraud the legitimate stamp collector/stamp dealer.

A postal counterfeit will be produced in quantity, profit for the perpetrator being in direct proportion to the number of items made, distributed and used in the mail. Naturally, the more that are distributed and sold, the greater the profit. The philatelic counterfeit is a single or limited production item; its value is dependent on the rarity factor, and is inversely related to quantity. The more of a given item produced, the lesser the value of each to the collector.

Fakes or philatelic forgeries are generally defined as genuine postage stamps that have been altered in some way that makes them more desirable or valuable to the collector or dealer. Stamp fakery or alteration usually involves physical or chemical manipulation of perforations, watermarks or condition. Like philatelic counterfeits, philatelic fakes or forgeries are aimed at stamp collectors or dealers. (Although some fakers create items for their own personal edification, at some point many of these items can and often do end up in the marketplace.)

A philatelic fake will involve one or more of the following:

1. Concealing/repairing a defect (e.g., a tear, a thin spot, a hinge mark).
2. Making an originally perforated stamp appear imperforate, or perforated in a way in which the original was not.
3. Altering a design, lettering, color, or denomination.
4. Making a stamp appear postmarked, overprinted, or used, or, conversely, removing cancels or other marks.
5. Repairing the gum or entirely regumming a stamp so it appears to be original.

A philatelic phantom or Cinderella is a fabrication, a sticker, and not a stamp. It is completely bogus, and unconnected with any legitimate postal authority's genuine issues.

Then there is the area of stamp reuse. This also is a form of counterfeiting. When someone removes a stamp that already has gone through the mail from its original envelope and then reuses it, or sells it for reuse by others, that someone has broken the law. The actual absence or removal of cancellation marks is immaterial – there is no validity to the argument that the post office failed to cancel the stamp, therefore it is "still good" and can be used again. The federal courts have ruled consistently that this is postal counterfeiting, and a violation of Title 18, United States Code, Section 501. To combat the defrauding of the post office through stamp reuse, the post office has been given both this counterfeiting statute and a misdemeanor statute (cancelled stamp and envelope, 18 USC 1720) to use in prosecutions.

The reuse of stamps by either business or the public is not the joke that it might first appear to be. For the Post Office it is like death by a thousand cuts. When individuals clip off an uncancelled stamp and put it on another envelope – it is no big deal. When enterprising individuals sense a business opportunity, and do this as a business, it is another story. Periodically this has happened in postal history, and it has cost the post office millions of dollars. It can be little old ladies as related below:

> She came into the post office and walked up to the parcel post window in a small town. Sweetly she asked the clerk if she could borrow the mucilage bottle. It was handed out. The clerk watched her paste two

stamps on the heavy parcel post package and she brought the package back to the window. He took one look at the stamps pasted on and said "forty cents please." "Why forty cents?" said the woman with anger. "Don't you see that there are two stamps of 20 cents each?" "I can't see it" said the clerk. "There is nothing on the package, for the two stamps have been used before and I advise you to produce forty cents for two good twenty cent stamps for I know that there is a fine of $100 for using cancelled stamps on packages over again." The forty cents was forthcoming and the clerk with one full sweep of his hand brushed the stamps the woman had put on the package into the waste basket. Looking up he saw and heard the door of the post office close with a load bang.

> Linn's Weekly Stamp News, October 12, 1935, p.946

Or it can be individuals who realize they can do this in volume and sell their product to others. When in the late '70s the Postal Service decided to seriously look for postage revenue fraud, an unexpected discovery was made. It was found that hundreds of individuals were conducting a thriving business in "ungummed - uncancelled" postage, a product not produced by the postal establishment since the 1930s. Go to any philatelic publication of the day and you will find numerous advertisements offering these items for sale.

Organized Crime
And the Art of Counterfeiting

There has always been crime in America. With the development of cities, individual criminality soon began to group into gangs. The organization of criminal activity really got its start in New York with Tammany Hall, which soon allied itself with the criminal class to control political power in the city. Gangs in many cases were ethnically divided – Irish, German, Jewish and Italian. Either through organizational skill or sheer ruthlessness the Italian/ Sicilians eventually became predominant. The wealth generated from controlling the flow of illegal alcohol and later, drugs, enabled what we identify today as organized crime to spread its tentacles throughout the country.

Either as a soldier (made member) or an associate, when you become part of this organization, your function in life is to make money. Postal revenue is simply another target to be exploited. You are continually looking for new ways to do this, both legally and otherwise. This keeps your bosses happy, and how successful you are at raising money determines what happens to you in your chosen career path. Not surprisingly, in the search for earnings, these folks time and again have turned to counterfeiting.

It is not known exactly when organized crime took aim at postal revenue, but since the very earliest days of organized crime these folks have been enthralled with the concept of literally making money. At the turn of the last century, Lupo the Wolf (Ignazio Lupo), a noted Black Hand killer, gained prominence not for the many killings he was involved in, but rather for setting up a counterfeit currency operation. He simply kidnapped two skilled printers, put them in a building, and told them they could not leave until the work was done.

Again and again these individuals would return to the world of the printing press. Usually it would not be with ink on their own hands, but with people they could intimidate, hire, or just buy finished products from. Many times when running down a stamp case, I would find that bogus cash was also involved. Sometimes the product produced was good, sometimes bad. With postage stamps, well, nobody looks at a stamp. Everyone looks at a $100 bill.

Based in Chicago, in my own battles, I spent years developing strings of informants that ranged from criminals to the cop on the beat. Sometimes it was difficult to tell one from another. Regardless, they kept me in the loop regarding what was going on. Interesting pieces of information would frequently surface. In one case the mob, with connections to a professional printer, simply gave the owner tickets to the Bahamas and told him to take a two-week vacation. While he was gone, they printed the stamps in his shop and then moved on.

Then there was a story I would hear off and on. There was this master printer who lived in Chicago. He was a guy who really knew his stuff. I remember hearing this story from two individuals involved in printing the Kennedy stamp. They actually were low-level "outfit" guys who had done the printing themselves. Jokingly they told me how they had honed their printing skills while guests of the government at Sandstone Federal Prison. With the 13-cent Kennedy, they had to do the printing, because the person who usually contracted for the mob's printing "was no longer available." In Jason Kersten's book *The Art of Making Money*, I think I found a little bit more of this story.[35]

Working as an independent, periodically "Divinci" would do a printing. Sometimes it was of stamps, usually currency. In his operation, he had strict rules that he followed. He would only print so much of a given item. He would never use or pass the items he printed himself. When he sold his product, it was with the understanding that it was never to be used or passed in his proximity. It was to be sent to other states. The story that Kersten related was that one day he went out to make a delivery and simply never returned. Most likely he lies in a shallow grave or his body was found in the trunk of a car. In the 1960s and 70s that was one of the mob's established ways to dump a body.

Historically, counterfeiting has been an art form. This has been an occupation requiring great skill and that commanded respect in the criminal's world. A breakthrough occurred with the introduction of the camera, moving criminal attention from the coin to paper. When it is in skilled hands, photo duplication allowed for easy copying. Then matching papers and inks added a final dimension. Still, to make acceptable copies it takes effort and attention to detail. Duplicating currency is difficult: You have the paper, multiple inks, the design work itself. The Treasury has been able to keep ahead of the general run-of-the mill counterfeiter, but the photocopy machine turned a new page in the book. For years the Treasury Department kept color copiers off of the market. Now throw in the attacks that appeared to be coming from hostile nation states (you pick the country) and something had to be done.

If the Secret Service was not busy enough combating the real counterfeiters who were craftsmen, now suddenly they were in the swamp, swatting clouds of mosquitoes: high school kids, janitors, you name it, decided they could make their own money. Then enter the "superbill" and the Treasury's hand was forced. To meet the new

---

35 *The Art of Making Money* is the best book on counterfeiting I have ever encountered. It tells the story of a counterfeiter from his point of view.

challenges, in the 1990s our currency was finally redesigned. In 2010 a new edition was rolled off the presses.

The issuance of new currency is timely. The amateurs have been a distraction, but the real problem has been the professional counterfeiters both in this country and overseas. A few years ago a press was taken down in Columbia that was producing nearly perfect bills. Then you have what was first dubbed the "superbill." I first encountered this item in the St. Paul Dead Letter Office. Postal employees opening letters to find a delivery address reported they were finding five or so $100 bills in envelopes. The source of these bills appeared to be the Middle East – Iran, Lebanon, Syria – pick a country. It did not take long for North Korea to also become identified as a new source. It is common knowledge that North Korea has been duplicating both our currency and stamps since the Korean conflict.

Little public information is known about the "superbill." With U.S. currency being the reserve currency for the world, the suspicion is there are billions of dollars in bogus U.S. currency stuffed into mattresses and buried in Mason jars around the world. Throw into the mix the two Asians caught crossing the Swiss border with suitcases full of nearly perfect Treasury bonds, and you begin to see the scope of the problem.

We still have the photocopy cowboys out there. You still have individuals using traditional printing methods who produce their product. The number of counterfeiters inside this country who have successfully duplicated the new currency you can count on the fingers of one hand. The same cannot be said for what is coming from other countries.

For the Post Office, what happened between 1895 and roughly 1940 was just a preliminary round. After 1940 postal revenue will be under major attack from many directions. Again, in many instances there will be a connection between both currency and stamps.